BEYOND THE SERMON:

Practical Lessons from Pulpit to Pew

Bishop Marshall D. Mays, D. Min

"Study to shew thyself approved unto God, a workman that needeth not to be ashamed, rightly dividing the word of truth."

II Timothy 2:15, KJV

Practical Christian Education Study Lessons for Practical Living

Scripture quotations as noted are from:

The Holy Bible, King James Version (KJV)
New International Version (NIV)

ISBN: 9798294559854 (Paperback)

ISBN: 9798294560263 (Hardcover)

Book design by Sunshine Marketing Solutions.

Printed by Sunshine Marketing Solutions, in the United States of America.

Sunshine Marketing Solutions
Lynchburg, VA 24502
Email: Elevate@marketingwithsunshine.com
Website: www.marketingwithsunshine.com

DEDICATION

This project is lovingly dedicated to my beautiful and devoted wife, Florence McDaniel Mays, my unwavering number one supporter. Her constant prayers, day and night, ensure I am physically, mentally, and spiritually prepared for every preaching and teaching moment.

To my five incredible daughters: Amy, April, Silisa, Catoria, and Janell—and to my ten energetic grandchildren and two precious great-grandchildren—you are my joy and my inspiration.

I also dedicate this work to the faithful Christian Education Ministries of:

- Otterville Baptist Church, Bedford, Virginia
- Ivy Hill Baptist Church, Monroe, Virginia
- St. Paul Baptist Church, Amherst, Virginia

In Cherished Memory

This project is offered in loving memory of those whose lives deeply impacted mine:

My beloved nephew, Delando Woody, who tirelessly ensured our family stayed connected and often gathered for joy and fellowship.

My loving, caring, and protecting sister, Annette Joanne Burford, who prayed for me and courageously defended me when others criticized her brother, the preacher.

My beloved brother-in-law, John Fuqua, was a true father figure who always recognized me as his pastor.

My awesome Deacons, Deacon J.W. Cheatwood and Deacon Robert Williams, and Bro. George Hurt, Jr, for their profound love and support for their Pastor and church, and for their faithful participation in the Otterville Baptist Church Christian Education Ministry.

FOREWORD

With immense joy and profound respect, I introduce "Beyond The Sermon: Practical Lessons from Pulpit to Pew," by my beloved brother in Christ, Bishop Marshall Mays, DMin. Having known Bishop Mays for over a decade, I've consistently been moved by his unwavering dedication to the spiritual growth of God's people. He's not just a gifted orator; he's a true shepherd with a heart deeply committed to equipping and empowering every individual in their faith journey.

Bishop Mays articulates so clearly the vital need he's brilliantly addressed with this work. He shares his passion for both preaching and teaching, a truth evident to anyone who has experienced his ministry. He invests countless hours delving into the Word, always with the singular goal of seeing lives transformed. His observation about the scarcity of "practical Christian education study lessons for everyday living" resonated deeply with me, as I'm sure it will with countless church leaders and members.

This book is a direct answer to that need. It's a testament to Bishop Mays's divine calling, providing accessible and tangible lessons that transcend the church walls, reaching individuals wherever they are. Whether you're a seasoned leader seeking fresh insights or just beginning your walk with the Lord, the wisdom within these pages will be a faithful companion, guiding you through life's challenges with biblical insight.

What you hold in your hands is more than just a book; it's a powerful tool for activation. It's Bishop Mays's heart poured onto every page, designed to empower you to live out your faith daily, practically, and boldly. I wholeheartedly commend this invaluable resource to you. Prepare to be inspired, equipped, and profoundly blessed.

With heartfelt admiration and blessing,

Dr. Andre Austin

A graduate of Boston University

ACKNOWLEDGMENTS

God has graced me to see 60 years in ministry, and this is the first book that I've come across that captures the varying issues that we all wrestle with during one season or another, and even greater, provides a solution. I highly recommend this book as a practical guide to navigate the various circumstances we must face in our Christian journey.

Bishop Marshall Mays' latest book, *Beyond The Sermon: Practical Lessons from Pulpit to Pew*, is a must-have tool for every believer who desires to mature in the faith and grow in the knowledge of Jesus Christ. This book contains 55 lessons that can be used over one year, at the rate of one lesson per week, to aid in your spiritual development. This great work of literature would also be an excellent resource for your family to study and discuss during your family devotion time.

Finally, it is an honor to acknowledge a true friend whom I hold in the highest esteem in academia and as a faith leader.

"Now to Him who is able to do exceedingly abundantly above all that we ask or think, according to the power that works in us, to Him be glory in the church by Christ Jesus to all generations, forever and ever. Amen." — Ephesians 3:20-21 NKJV

Bishop Carroll A. Baltimore
Presiding Prelate, Ecumenical Global Mission Alliance

PREFACE

I'm passionate about both preaching and teaching. A significant part of my ministry is dedicated to diligently studying and preparing sermons and lessons to empower the congregation I serve. After leading numerous Christian education studies, I often reflect on the availability of resources, specifically, books offering practical lessons designed to inspire and assist church leaders and members in their daily walk with the Lord.

While the market is rich with theological texts and guides on designing biblical curricula, there's a noticeable gap in practical Christian education study lessons for everyday living. God placed this project on my heart to provide church leaders and members with accessible, tangible Christian education lessons they can study, especially when they're unable to attend mid-week Bible study or Sunday School.

The material within this book is intended to be both instructive and suggestive. While the majority of the content is my original work, I humbly acknowledge my indebtedness to many sources that have informed my understanding and presentation.

Bishop Marshall D. Mays, D. Min

TABLE OF CONTENTS

Practical Lessons

Lesson 1
Don't Abort Your
God-Given Purpose

Scripture: Nehemiah 6:1-9

The Book of Nehemiah is a powerful historical account in Scripture that highlights the return of the Israelites from Babylonian captivity and the rebuilding of Jerusalem. Nehemiah, a Jewish man serving in Persia, became deeply burdened when he heard that although the Temple was being restored, the walls of Jerusalem remained in ruins, leaving the city vulnerable and exposed.

Nehemiah's response was not passive. He prayed earnestly, asking God for permission and provision to return and rebuild the walls. God answered his prayer by softening the heart of King Artaxerxes, who not only granted Nehemiah leave to return to Jerusalem but also supplied him with timber and official letters of support. This moment reminds us that when God gives you a purpose, He will also align people and resources to help you fulfill it. Divine assignments are rarely solo missions, and God often works through others to help bring your calling to life.

But with every God-ordained purpose comes opposition. Satan, the enemy of your soul, is strategic. He works to persuade you to give up, abandon, or delay the assignment God has placed in your hands. In Nehemiah chapter 6, we uncover three life-giving

2

principles that can help you guard your purpose from spiritual sabotage.

Principle 1: Don't Negotiate with the Enemy (v.1-4)

When Nehemiah's enemies, Sanballat, Tobiah, Geshem the Arab, and others, realized the wall was nearly complete and only the gates remained, they launched a subtle attack. Instead of coming with swords, they sent an invitation. "Come, let us meet together in one of the villages on the plain of Ono," they said. But Nehemiah discerned the true intent behind their message. They were planning to harm him.

Nehemiah's response was simple and direct: "I am carrying on a great project and cannot go down." He knew that leaving the wall, even for a conversation, would disrupt the progress and allow his enemies to sabotage the work. They sent the same message four times, and each time, Nehemiah gave the same unwavering answer.

This moment reveals something critical about the nature of spiritual attacks. The enemy often won't attack your purpose head-on; instead, he'll try to distract you with invitations, meetings, and conversations that seem harmless but are designed to pull you away from your assignment. It may come in the form of opportunities that appear promising but aren't aligned with your calling. Or it may be people who want your attention, not to support your vision, but to slow it down.

When you're walking for a divine purpose, you must recognize that not every invitation deserves a response. Some doors are meant to be ignored. The more focused you are, the less time you have for fruitless distractions. Just as Nehemiah stayed on the wall, we too must stay planted in our purpose and refuse to negotiate with anything or anyone that pulls us away from it.

Principle 2: Don't Give in to Intimidation (v.5-9):

When Nehemiah's enemies failed to pull him away through negotiation, they didn't give up. They simply changed their approach. What couldn't be accomplished through distraction, they now attempted through fear. Their next strategy was intimidation.

"Then, the fifth time, Sanballat sent his aide to me with the same message, and in his hand was an unsealed letter." This wasn't a private conversation. It was a public attack. An unsealed letter meant its contents could easily be read and spread among others. It was a deliberate move to stir rumors and plant seeds of doubt among the people.

Inside the letter were bold and dangerous accusations: "It is reported among the nations and Geshem says it is true that you and the Jews are plotting to revolt, and therefore you are building the wall. Moreover, according to these reports, you are about to become their king and have even appointed prophets to make this proclamation about you in Jerusalem: 'There is a king in Judah!' Now this report will get back to the king; so, come, let us meet together."

This was no idle threat. Sanballat and his allies were implying that Nehemiah was planning to rebel against Persia and crown himself king. These kinds of rumors could have easily turned deadly. The goal was

4

to frighten Nehemiah into abandoning the work and to make him feel exposed, accused, and vulnerable. This is exactly how the enemy operates. When distraction doesn't work, he tries to shake your confidence with lies, slander, and threats.

But Nehemiah didn't panic. He didn't allow fear to dictate his next move. Instead, he stood firm and responded directly: "Nothing like what you are saying is happening; you are just making it up out of your own head." He didn't try to defend his reputation to everyone who might have heard the rumor. He didn't let the pressure push him off course. He confronted the lie, exposed its falsehood, and kept moving forward.

Nehemiah's confidence wasn't in his own strength. It was in his connection to God. He recognized what the enemy was really after: "They were all trying to frighten us, thinking, 'Their hands will get too weak for the work, and it will not be completed.'" Their plan was clear: wear down the workers' resolve, paralyze them with fear, and bring the project to a stop.

But Nehemiah knew precisely how to respond in moments like this. He didn't lash out. He didn't run. He prayed. "But I prayed, 'Now strengthen my hands.'" (v.9b) In the face of intimidation, Nehemiah went straight to the source of his strength—God.

This principle is powerful for us today. When we are walking in purpose, we will face moments where fear tries to creep in. It may come in the form of criticism, gossip, personal attacks, or even spiritual doubt. The goal is always the same: to weaken your hands and stop the work.

But just like Nehemiah, you don't have to give fear the final word. Speak truth to the lies. Stand firm in your calling. And when you feel pressure closing in, pause and pray, "Lord, strengthen my hands."

Fear may come, but it doesn't have to win. Your assignment is too important to abandon. Stay focused. Stay grounded. And let God strengthen you to finish the work He's called you to do.

Principle 3: Always Pray and Ask God for Strength (v.9):

After all the threats, lies, and intimidation tactics, Nehemiah still refused to be shaken. He didn't allow fear to weaken his resolve or distract him from the assignment God had given him. He understood that the battle wasn't just physical. It was spiritual. And in moments like these, he turned to his greatest weapon: prayer.

Nehemiah didn't fold. He didn't let the weight of the pressure cause him to collapse under fear. Even when he was surrounded by opposition and under public scrutiny, he stood firm.

He didn't give up. There were many reasons to walk away. The threats were real, the accusations dangerous, and the emotional toll heavy, but Nehemiah pressed on with perseverance.

He didn't throw in the towel. He didn't abandon the work or delay his progress just because things got difficult. He didn't retreat to safety or compromise his position to gain peace. Instead, he stayed in the fight, committed to the mission.

He prayed. He didn't try to strategize his way out of fear or rely on his leadership skills alone. He turned to God and cried out for help. In verse 9, he says: "They were all trying to frighten us, thinking, 'Their hands will get too weak for the work, and it will not be completed.' But I prayed, 'Now strengthen my hands.'"

This simple but powerful prayer reveals the heart of a man who knew where his strength truly came from. Nehemiah was not only a builder. He was a man of prayer. Throughout the book that bears his name, we see him praying repeatedly: when he hears bad news, when he needs favor, when facing resistance, and when needing strength. Prayer wasn't a last resort. It was his daily rhythm. It was his lifeline.

He understood that staying focused on purpose requires more than determination. It requires divine strength, the strength that only comes through prayer. Through his ongoing conversation with God, Nehemiah was able to resist distractions, overcome intimidation, and finish what he started.

We, too, will face moments when our hands feel weak. The pressure may be great, the obstacles heavy, and the voices around us loud. But like Nehemiah, we must respond by turning to God, not just with complaints, but with a specific request: "Lord, strengthen my hands."

Final Word:

You were created with purpose. Your life is not random, and your calling is not accidental. God assigned you to a specific work: a divine assignment that carries eternal value. But with purpose comes pressure. And with calling comes conflict. The enemy doesn't fight what isn't a threat. So, if you're feeling opposition, be encouraged because it's often a sign that you're right where God wants you.

Just like Nehemiah, you may face moments where you're tempted to come down from the wall. Distractions will come disguised as invitations. Negotiations will seem harmless. Intimidation will arrive in the form of rumors, pressure, and fear. And when distractions don't stop you, the enemy will try to wear you down emotionally, mentally, and spiritually.

You must stay focused. Stay faithful. Stay on the wall. Don't let fear speak louder than your calling. Don't let discouragement stop what God has started in you. Nehemiah refused to abandon his assignment because he knew the work was excellent. And so is yours.

When it gets hard and it will, pray like Nehemiah did: "Now strengthen my hands." God is not asking you to finish in your own strength. He is ready to empower you, to carry you, and to equip you with everything you need to fulfill His purpose for your life.

So don't abort your God-given assignment. Fulfill it with focus, courage, and prayer. Stand firm. Keep building. And trust that the same God who gave you the vision will provide you with the strength to complete it.

Lesson 2
Growing in Grace

Scripture: II Peter 3:18

God: The Source of All Grace

The Creator of the universe, the only wise, true, and living God, is not only the Maker of all things but also the rightful Owner of everything that exists. Psalm 24:1–2 reminds us, "The earth is the Lord's, and everything in it, the world, and all who live in it; for He founded it on the seas and established it on the waters." The God we serve is not distant. He is actively present, full of grace, mercy, and unwavering love.

His character reveals His nature. God is loving. His love is unconditional and constant. He is compassionate. He feels our pain and draws near in our weakness. He is affectionate, caring deeply about the details of our lives. He is kind, showing mercy even when we deserve judgment. And He faithfully surrounds us with His favor and care every day. Yet God's intent is not just for us to receive His grace, but to grow in it. As II Peter 3:18 instructs, we are to "grow in the grace and knowledge of our Lord and Savior Jesus Christ."

What Is Grace?

Grace, in its simplest form, is God's unmerited favor. It is His goodness extended to us without condition or cause. Grace is God loving us even when we fall short. He decides to bless us when we've done nothing to earn it. It is God choosing mercy over punishment, provision over lack, and faithfulness over frustration.

This grace is not occasional. It is constant. Jeremiah captures this beautifully in Lamentations 3:22-23: "It is of the Lord's mercies that we are not consumed, because his compassions fail not. They are new every morning: great is thy faithfulness." In the midst of national devastation, Jeremiah didn't lose sight of God's enduring mercy. Each day, God's grace arrives fresh and sufficient.

This truth also echoes through the lyrics of a timeless hymn:
"Great is Thy faithfulness, O God my Father.
There is no shadow of turning with Thee...
Morning by morning, new mercies I see.
All I have needed Thy hand hath provided."

Isaiah speaks similarly in Isaiah 63:7, "I will tell of the kindnesses of the Lord... according to all the Lord has done for us." From generation to generation, God's mercy has no expiration. It is always available, always present, always enough.

What It Means to Grow in Grace

When Peter writes that we must grow in grace, he's not simply encouraging us to become more religious. He is calling for spiritual maturity, a growth that goes beyond head knowledge into life transformation. It is not about memorizing facts about Jesus but about becoming more like Him in heart, thought, and action.

To grow in grace means to move beyond spiritual infancy. It means maturing in our character, deepening in our faith, and growing in wisdom. It means letting go of spiritual complacency and allowing God to shape us daily through His Word and Spirit. Hebrews 4:16 calls us to draw near to God's throne boldly because His grace is always available to help us in our time of need.

Growing in Grace Requires Growing in the Word of God

The foundation of grace-filled living begins with God's Word. It is through Scripture that we learn who God is, what He has done, and how we are to live in response. Studying the Word is not just about quoting verses. It's about transformation.

When we grow in the Word, we begin to see God more clearly. We feast on His truth until it becomes the guide for our thoughts, actions, and decisions. Psalm 119:105 says, "Your word is a lamp to my feet and a light to my path." The Word shows us how to walk when life gets dark, how to stand when challenges come, and how to grow when pressure mounts.

Spiritual growth begins with Scripture. You cannot grow in grace without immersing yourself in the Word of God and allowing that Word to dwell in you richly.

Growing in Grace Requires Growing in Prayer

Prayer is the lifeline of every believer. It is through prayer that we commune with God, listen for His voice, and pour out our hearts. Growing in grace means developing a life of consistent, meaningful prayer.

Jesus taught in Luke 18:1 that we "should always pray and not give up." Paul echoed this in I Thessalonians 5:17: "Pray without ceasing." A growing prayer life deepens our trust in God. It strengthens our dependence on Him and allows us to experience His presence in real time.

Prayer is not a spiritual performance. It's an ongoing relationship. When we talk to God regularly, we invite His grace to shape us, comfort us, correct us, and lead us. A shallow prayer life limits our growth. A surrendered, open prayer life accelerates it.

Growing in Grace Requires Daily Surrender to the Lord

True spiritual growth cannot happen without surrender. Growing in grace means laying down your own will and embracing God's will instead. It means trusting His direction, even when it's difficult. Surrender is not weakness. It is a strength under submission.

In Romans 12:1, Paul writes, "I urge you… to present your bodies as a living sacrifice, holy and pleasing to God—this is your true and proper worship." Surrender means giving God all of you, your time, your desires, your future. It is a daily decision to follow

Jesus, even when your flesh wants to go a different direction.

Grace thrives in surrendered hearts. When we yield ourselves to Christ, we open the door for growth, for strength, and for greater intimacy with Him.

Final Word: A Song of Surrender

The message of this lesson is captured in the timeless hymn of surrender:

All to Jesus I surrender,
All to Him I freely give;
I will ever love and trust Him,
In His presence, daily live.
All to Jesus I surrender,
Lord, I give myself to Thee;
Fill me with Thy love and power,
Let Thy blessing fall on me.
I surrender all,
I surrender all;
All to Thee, my blessed Savior,
I surrender all.

To grow in grace is to walk with Jesus, not just occasionally, but daily. It is a life of trust, transformation, and total dependence on Him. May we never stop growing in the grace that saves us, sustains us, and calls us forward.

Lesson 3
Temptation:
You Can Overcome

Scripture: James 1:12 thru 14

Understanding the Reality of Temptation

Temptation is a universal challenge. Whether you've been walking with God for a short time or for decades, the enemy continues to look for moments of weakness to pull you off course. Scripture is clear: believers are not exempt from temptation, but we are empowered to overcome it.

The apostle Peter offers this sobering reminder in I Peter 5:8: "Be alert and of sober mind. Your enemy, the devil, prowls around like a roaring lion looking for someone to devour." The mission of Satan is also echoed by Jesus Himself in John 10:10, where He says, "The thief comes only to steal and kill and destroy; I have come that they may have life, and have it to the full."

We must not be ignorant of the enemy's tactics. Temptation is one of its oldest and most effective tools. But while temptation is inevitable, falling into sin is not. God has given us everything we need to recognize, resist, and rise above temptation.

What Is Temptation?

In the biblical context, temptation is an external enticement, a lure or invitation to sin, used by Satan to draw followers of Christ away from obedience and into rebellion. The goal of temptation is not just moral failure. It is spiritual separation. The enemy wants to erode our trust in God and dull our sensitivity to His voice.

James 1:14 tells us, "But each person is tempted when they are dragged away by their own evil desire and enticed." This means temptation works by appealing to our desires, twisting them just enough to make sin look satisfying. But God's Word equips us with wisdom and power to overcome.

Lesson 1: When Tempted by the Flesh—Flee

One of the most well-known examples of resisting temptation is found in the story of Joseph. In Genesis 39, Joseph is confronted by Potiphar's wife, who repeatedly tries to seduce him. Yet Joseph refuses to compromise. When the temptation becomes physically aggressive, Scripture says, "he left his cloak in her hand and ran out of the house." (Gen. 39:12)

Joseph didn't pause to weigh the pros and cons. He didn't stay to explain himself. He ran. He understood that staying in the presence of temptation increases the risk of falling. His immediate escape protected not only his integrity but also his future.

There is power in fleeing. Sometimes victory doesn't look like standing your ground. It looks like it is getting out of the room. The flesh craves what feels good in the moment, but faith prioritizes what honors God long-term. Like Joseph, you can overcome the temptation of the flesh when you choose flight over failure. When the temptation is too close, don't argue with it. Run from it.

Lesson 2: When Tempted by the World—Implement Your Faith

Temptation doesn't always come through blatant sin. Often, it's subtle and wrapped in cultural norms, worldly values, and attractive distractions. First John 2:15 warns us, "Do not love the world or anything in the world. If anyone loves the world, love for the Father is not in them."

To be entangled with the world is to become desensitized to God. The lust of the flesh, the lust of the eyes, and the pride of life can slowly pull us away from spiritual focus and reorient our affections toward temporary things. Overcoming this kind of temptation requires more than just avoidance. It requires action. You must implement your faith.

To "walk by faith and not by sight" (II Corinthians 5:7) means you measure decisions not by what is popular, but by what pleases God. You filter opportunities, relationships, and ambitions through the lens of the Word. You remind yourself that what looks appealing in the world's eyes may not align with God's will.

Faith is not passive. It's a daily discipline. When temptation comes dressed in worldly success, comfort, or compromise, activate your faith. Stand firm on the promises of God and let your convictions lead your choices.

Lesson 3: When Tempted by the Devil—Resist

Not all temptation comes through the flesh or the world. Sometimes, the source is a direct spiritual attack. The enemy is bold and relentless, but he is also defeated. James 4:7 offers a powerful instruction and promise: "Submit yourselves, then, to God. Resist the devil, and he will flee from you."

To resist the devil means to take a stand. It means to refuse his lies, reject his pressure, and rebuke his influence over your life. But resistance is only effective when it's rooted in submission to God. You can't fight the enemy with your own strength. You must first come under the authority of Christ.

Jesus demonstrated this during His temptation in the wilderness. Each time Satan tempted Him, Jesus responded with, "It is written…" He countered every lie with the truth of God's Word. That's our blueprint. Know the Word. Speak the Word. Stand on the Word.

When the devil comes after you, resist him and he will flee. He has no power over a believer who is submitted to God and armed with Scripture. Victory is not found in fear but in faith-fueled resistance.

Final Word

Temptation is real. It's relentless. And it shows up in many forms. But no matter how strong it seems, you can overcome it. Whether it's the lure of the flesh, the pull of the world, or the schemes of the devil, you are not powerless. God has given you tools: His Word, His Spirit, and His strength to stand firm.

The old hymn still holds true:

> "*Yield not to temptation, for yielding is sin.*
>
> *Each victory will help you some other to win.*
>
> *Fight manfully onward, dark passions subdue.*
>
> *Look ever to Jesus, and He will carry you through.*"

You were not called to be perfect. But you were empowered to be victorious. The more you walk with Christ, the stronger you become. Temptation may knock, but you don't have to open the door. Look to Jesus, rely on His strength, and keep pressing forward. You can overcome.

Lesson 4
Evil Thoughts and Behavior Is a Sin

Scripture: Proverbs 24:19-20

The Power of Our Thoughts

In his book Naked and Not Ashamed, Bishop T.D. Jakes writes, "Your thoughts are often the product of damaged emotions, traumatic events, and vicious opinions forced upon you by domineering people who continually feel it necessary to express their opinion about you." That insight exposes a deep truth: our thought life is shaped not just by what happens to us, but by how we process it.

Too often, we allow the harsh words and criticisms of others to define us. But at the end of the day, what truly matters is not what others think or say, it's how God sees us. Living to please people rather than God is not just unwise. It's sinful. Acts 5:29 reminds us that "We must obey God rather than human beings," and Galatians 1:10 challenges us to ask: "Am I now trying to win the approval of human beings, or of God?"

Many evil thoughts are rooted in past wounds: offenses, betrayals, disappointments. Some people carry the weight of their yesterday into every part of their today. They become bitter, angry, short-tempered, and even vengeful because they've refused to release what hurt them. But God never designed us to live imprisoned by our past. He calls us to be renewed in our minds and transformed by His truth.

Lesson 1: Understand How God Sees Evil Thoughts (Proverbs 15:26)

God is not indifferent to what we think. Proverbs 15:26 says, "The Lord detests the thoughts of the wicked, but gracious words are pure in His sight." Evil thoughts aren't neutral. They are offensive to a holy God. They don't just damage our perspective; they stain our spirit.

Scripture also teaches that as a man thinks in his heart, so is he (Proverbs 23:7). In other words, our thoughts shape our identity. If you constantly dwell on bitterness, hatred, jealousy, or vengeance, those thoughts eventually define your words and actions. What lives in the heart finds its way to the mouth, and Jesus said, "For by your words you will be acquitted, and by your words you will be condemned."

Evil thoughts, left unchecked, will eventually manifest in behavior. That's why transformation begins in the mind. Renewing your mind with God's truth is the first step to breaking free from destructive patterns.

Lesson 2: Forsake Wickedness and Unrighteousness (Isaiah 55:7)

To forsake something means to abandon it and to turn away completely. Isaiah 55:7 says, "Let the wicked forsake their ways and the unrighteous their thoughts. Let them turn to the Lord, and He will have mercy on them, and to our God, for He will freely pardon."

Walking with Christ requires not only avoiding sinful actions but also rejecting the thought patterns that lead to those actions. When we cling to wickedness in our hearts, we forfeit the blessings of obedience. The Bible is filled with examples of people who missed out on God's best because they held on to pride, selfishness, or rebellion.

Moses, though deeply faithful, allowed his anger to override his obedience. As a result, he was not permitted to enter the Promised Land (Numbers 20:7–12; Deuteronomy 34:1–7).

The rich man in Luke 16 ignored the needs of Lazarus, a poor beggar at his gate. His selfishness led to eternal separation from God (Luke 16:19–23).

King Herod Agrippa I, in Acts 12:23, was struck down and eaten by worms because he accepted praise that belonged to God and refused to give Him glory.

Sinful thoughts left unchecked become sinful behavior. But God, in His mercy, invites us to forsake every wicked way and come back to Him.

Proverbs 28:13 reinforces this truth: "Whoever conceals their sins does not prosper, but the one who confesses and renounces them finds mercy." God doesn't expect perfection, but He does require repentance. Mercy is always available, but only to those who are willing to surrender.

Lesson 3: Return to the Lord (Isaiah 55:7)

Returning to the Lord begins with repentance. Repentance is more than just feeling bad about your actions. It's a heartfelt turning back to God. It's admitting that your way didn't work and choosing to follow His way instead.

King David modeled this powerfully in Psalm 51. After falling into sin, he came to God with brokenness and honesty: "Create in me a clean heart, O God, and renew a right spirit within me... Restore to me the joy of your salvation." (Psalm 51:10–12)

Likewise, the Prodigal Son, in Luke 15, recognized his sin, humbled himself, and said to his father, "I have sinned against heaven and against you." That act of repentance opened the door to restoration.

When we return to God, He doesn't meet us with condemnation. He meets us with compassion. He restores what was broken and replaces toxic thoughts with praise. He heals the wounds that once fueled bitterness and gives us a renewed mind, filled with hope, peace, and purpose.

Final Word: From Evil Thoughts to Everlasting Praise

The journey away from evil thoughts begins with honesty. We must recognize the poison in our hearts, release the past that tries to define us, and return to the God who can renew us.

Psalm 34:1 says, "I will bless the Lord at all times; His praise shall continually be in my mouth." That kind of praise is only possible when your heart is right with God.

If you're struggling with anger, resentment, jealousy, or bitterness, know this: you don't have to stay there. You can be free. Let go of the past. Release the opinions of others. Surrender every evil thought and allow the Lord to renew your mind.

When you return to God, like David, your heart will overflow with praise, not pain. And you'll walk in the peace and freedom that only comes from Him.

Lesson 5
The Need to Renew Our Vision

Scripture: Proverbs 29:18; II Timothy 1:1-8

Why Vision Matters

Solomon, the wise preacher, teaches that it is impossible to succeed in life or ministry without vision. Proverbs 29:18 states, "Where there is no vision, the people perish." Vision is not a luxury—it is a necessity. Whether in your personal life or in the church, vision provides purpose, focus, and forward momentum. Without it, efforts become scattered, growth stalls, and the mission eventually dies. Vision is what moves a person or a community from what it is to what it could be. It breathes life into plans and gives clarity to calling.

What Is Vision?

Vision is more than a goal. It is a spiritual insight into the future. It enables us to see beyond present challenges and dream with God. Vision is the bridge between where we are and where God is calling us to go. It is hope with a plan. Vision sparks invention, inspires mothers to believe in their children, and gives leaders the ability to see the unseen. It motivates ministry and fuels purpose. Without vision, people settle for survival instead of pursuing divine significance.

Apostle Paul's second letter to Timothy highlights areas where vision is needed most. His words serve as both encouragement and instruction. As Paul nears the end of his earthly ministry, he urges Timothy and us to rekindle our vision for worship, prayer, and outreach. These are not optional ministries. They are central to the health and effectiveness of every believer and every church.

Renew Our Vision for Worship (II Timothy 1:1-3; Psa. 95:6):

Paul opens his letter with a powerful example of what it means to live a life of worship. In 2 Timothy 1:1-3, he describes how he has served God with a clear conscience, just as his ancestors did. Paul's worship was not limited to church services or sacred moments—it was a lifestyle. Everything he did was an offering to God. Psalm 95:6 invites us into that same posture: "Come, let us bow down in worship, let us kneel before the Lord our Maker."

To renew our vision for worship, we must embrace a life of daily devotion to God. Worship is not confined to music or moments; it is an expression of love, loyalty, and reverence toward the Creator. It is celebrating the goodness of God not just on Sundays, but every day, through our choices, our words, and our obedience. When we view worship as a way of life, we step into a deeper, more authentic relationship with God.

Renew Our Vision for Prayer (II Timothy 1:4-5):

In verses 3–5, Paul reflects on his continual prayers for Timothy. He doesn't offer a formula or a technique. Instead, he models heartfelt intercession. Paul's prayer life flowed from his concern and love. He poured out his heart to God. There was no performance. It was just a relationship.

Luke 18:1 reminds us that we "should always pray and not give up." Romans 10:1 echoes Paul's desire for others to experience salvation. To renew our vision for prayer, we must return to that place of sincerity and depth. Prayer is not about eloquence or routine. It is about vulnerability and trust. When the church embraces its identity as a house of prayer, every ministry gains power. Every plan becomes rooted in God's will. And every believer grows in intimacy with the Father.

Renew Our Vision for Outreach (II Timothy 1:8a):

In 2 Timothy 1:8, Paul encourages Timothy not to be ashamed of the testimony of Jesus Christ. This call to boldness is a call to outreach. Outreach is the heartbeat of the gospel. Jesus didn't just call His disciples to stay in the temple. He sent them into the world. In Matthew 28:19-20 and Mark 16:15, the Great Commission is clear: make disciples, preach the good news, and reach the lost.

Renewing our vision for outreach requires courage and compassion. It means testifying about what God has done in our lives and extending His love to others. Acts 1:8 says we are to be witnesses—starting where we are and expanding outward. The church must remain committed to reaching those who are far from God. We do this through service, evangelism, and authentic relationships. When we renew our passion for outreach, the church regains its urgency and relevance in a hurtful world.

Final Word:

P.K. Bernard once said, "A man without a vision is a man without a future. A man without a future will always return to his past." Without vision, there is no direction. Without direction, we drift. And when we drift, we often end up back in old places that God has already delivered us from.

But when God renews your vision, He revives your purpose. He sharpens your focus and reminds you of the calling He placed on your life. Today, ask God to renew your vision for worship, for prayer, and for outreach. Let Him stir up new dreams and reignite your passion to serve. When your vision is clear, your steps become steady, your mission becomes urgent, and your future becomes bright.

Lesson 6
Selfishness

Scripture: Luke 9:23

Understanding Selfishness

Selfishness is a destructive mindset that elevates personal desires above the needs of others. It causes spiritual stagnation and emotional harm, both to us and those around us. In Mark 8:36-37, Jesus warned that gaining the world while losing your soul is a loss of eternal proportions. This principle strikes at the heart of selfishness. It may offer temporary satisfaction, but ultimately it leads to spiritual emptiness.

Scripture consistently teaches that selfishness is not compatible with a Christ-centered life. James 4:3 tells us that unanswered prayers often stem from selfish motives. When our focus is self-serving rather than God-serving, we block the flow of God's power and provision. The Bible provides many descriptions for selfishness: self-centeredness, arrogance, self-importance, and vain conceit. Regardless of the specific term, they all describe the same root issue: living for self instead of living for God.

Is Selfishness a Sin?

The answer is yes. Selfishness is indeed a sin. Human beings are born with a natural tendency toward egocentrism, but we are not called to stay that way. As Christians, we are commanded to deny ourselves and follow Christ (Luke 9:23). Philippians 2:3 urges us to "do nothing out of selfish ambition or vain conceit. Rather, in humility value others above yourselves."

Sin, at its core, is about selfishness. It is choosing our will over God's will, indulging in what we desire regardless of the consequences. But Jesus provides a better way. His life was the model of selflessness, sacrifice, and love. As followers of Christ, we are empowered to overcome the pull of selfishness and embrace a life of surrender and service.

The Effects of Selfishness

Selfishness carries real and lasting consequences. James 3:16 teaches that where there is envy and selfish ambition, there will also be disorder and every evil practice. A selfish heart creates spiritual instability. It leads to frustration, bitterness, and a deep sense of emptiness. People who live selfishly often find themselves disconnected from God and unable to grow spiritually.

Selfishness also damages relationships. It manifests in small ways like speaking without thinking, shirking responsibilities, or constantly prioritizing one's own needs. It can also show up as internal resentment, jealousy, or entitlement. These attitudes rob us of joy and hinder the flow of love in our lives. God will not bless a double-minded heart that tries to serve self and Him at the same time (James 4:8; Revelation 3:16).

Selfishness in Scripture

The Bible offers numerous warnings and examples of selfishness. Cain's jealousy and self-focus led him to murder his brother Abel (Genesis 4). David's pursuit of personal pleasure with Bathsheba led to deceit and the death of an innocent man (2 Samuel 11). James and John asked Jesus for the most prestigious seats in His kingdom, not out of humility, but out of personal ambition (Matthew 20). Jesus quickly reminded them that true greatness comes through serving others.

Another striking example is the older brother in the story of the Prodigal Son (Luke 15). Though he remained physically close to the father, his selfish and bitter attitude revealed a heart far from grace. Scripture teaches that we cannot love God while harboring selfishness and refusing to love our brothers (1 John 4:20-21).

The Dangers of Self-Centered Living

Selfishness wears many masks, including self-conceit, self-righteousness, self-will, self-indulgence, and self-satisfaction. Each of these attitudes hinders spiritual growth and displeases God. Self-conceit causes people to overestimate their value and ignore correction. Self-righteousness, a common trait among the Pharisees, blinds individuals to their own sin while condemning others (Luke 18:9-14). Self-will leads to rebellion, as seen in those who stoned Stephen because they refused to surrender to God's truth (Acts 7:51-53).

Self-indulgence tempts believers to forsake spiritual discipline for temporary pleasure. Demas, once a faithful companion of Paul, abandoned his ministry because he loved the pleasures of the world more than the call of Christ (2 Timothy 4:10). Lastly, self-satisfaction or being contented with our spiritual state leads to complacency. Romans 8:5-8 warns that living to please the flesh makes us hostile to God.

Combating Selfishness Through Gratitude

The Psalms offer powerful tools to help us fight against selfishness. Psalm 136 calls us to give thanks to the Lord, remembering all He has done. Psalm 92:1 teaches us that gratitude should be our daily posture. Psalm 104 reminds us that everything we have comes from God. When we shift our focus from what we lack to all we have received, selfishness loses its grip. Gratitude re-centers our hearts and reawakens our compassion for others.

Terms to Remember:

Self-centeredness - This occurs when a person is absorbed in self. No one enjoys a self-centered person.

Self-conceit - This is an exaggerated estimation of one's own ability or powers, an overconfidence in oneself. God hates pride and resists the proud (Prov. 16:18; Jas. 4:6, 10; Lk. 18:14; Rom. 12:3).

Self-willed - One who is self-willed is stubborn, set on having his own way. Stiff-necked uncircumcised Jews stoned Stephen to death (Acts 7:51-53). They stubbornly clung to their own will rather than submitting to the will of God.

Self-indulgence - This is giving free course to one's own passions and inclinations. Self-indulgence is a sin that leads one away from God. Demas, who had once been a faithful disciple and co-worker of the apostle Paul, forsook the Lord and the apostle because he loved the present world and indulged himself in its pleasures (II Tim. 4:10).

Self-righteousness - This is being righteous in one's own eyes. It was a trait of the Pharisees (Lk. 18:9 -14; Rom. 10:1-3). It prompted them to accuse Jesus of eating with sinners (Matt. 9:10-12). They could see everyone's sins, but they could not see their own sins. To be pleasing to God, one must humbly acknowledge his own sinfulness (Psa. 51:3).

Self-satisfaction – The person who is pleased with who they are. The satisfied person has reached their goal. He has no other worlds to conquer, no loftier heights to scale, and no greater work to do. His journey can only be downward (Rom. 8:5-8).

Final Word: Living Beyond Yourself

The Christian life is not about self-fulfillment. It's about self-denial. Luke 9:23 offers the key to spiritual victory: "Whoever wants to be my disciple must deny themselves and take up their cross daily and follow me." God calls us to put aside selfish ambition, to think less about ourselves, and more about others.

Let the Word of God guide your thoughts, your words, and your actions. Ask Him daily to search your heart, remove selfishness, and fill you with His Spirit. You were not created to live for yourself. You were created to reflect Christ. And when you deny self and live for Him, you will discover the fullness of joy, purpose, and power that only comes through surrender.

Lesson 7
What Must I Do to Inherit Eternal Life

Scripture: Mark 10:17-22

The Rich Young Ruler

The man who fell on his knees before Jesus appeared to have everything one could want. Mark tells us that he was wealthy (Mark 10:22). Luke adds that he was a ruler, a man of influence and power (Luke 18:18). Matthew reveals that he was young (Matthew 19:20, 22). By all accounts, this man had the kind of life many people dream about. He was young, rich, and powerful. Yet despite his impressive status, he came to Jesus with an emptiness he could not ignore. He had gained wealth, influence, and success, but he still lacked the one thing that mattered most: eternal life.

Although he had everything money could buy and power could achieve, his soul was unsettled. He knew something was missing. He recognized that what he possessed could not satisfy the deepest longings of his heart. He realized there must be something more, something greater than what his wealth and influence could provide. That is why he came to Jesus, asking the most important question anyone could ask: "What must I do to inherit eternal life?"

The Longing for More

This man's desperation reminds us of a timeless truth. Sooner or later, the best the world offers proves insufficient. Riches fade, power weakens, youth disappears, and achievements lose their shine. Life on this earth is temporary, and deep within each of us there is a longing for more. Life is like a vapor that appears for a little while and then vanishes. God has placed eternity in the human heart, and no amount of earthly success can replace the eternal relationship He offers us.

The rich young ruler sensed this. He recognized that his possessions could not purchase eternal peace. He was drawn to Jesus because he wanted more than the world could give. Yet when confronted with the cost of discipleship, he struggled to let go of what bound him.

Jesus gave the man a clear response. If he genuinely wanted eternal life, there were three steps he needed to take.

Know the Commandments

Jesus first reminded the man of the commandments. To know the commandments is more than intellectual awareness. It is obedience to them. James, the half-brother of Jesus, made it clear that knowing what is right but refusing to do it is sin (James 4:17). Sin is not only committing what is wrong but also neglecting to do what is right. It is trespassing against

God's law by stepping into places or activities He has warned us to avoid.

To walk rightly with God requires acknowledging His commandments and seeking forgiveness when we fall short. Matthew 6 and Luke 11 record Jesus' teaching on prayer, where He instructs us to ask God for forgiveness and to extend forgiveness to others. Eternal life is not earned by keeping the law perfectly, but a heart that loves God seeks to honor His commands and walk in obedience.

Separate Yourself from What You Value More than God

The second instruction Jesus gave was far more personal. He told the rich young ruler to sell what he had and give to the poor, and then to follow Him. This was not a condemnation of wealth in itself but a revelation of the man's heart. His possessions had become more important than his relationship with God. He was rich in material goods but poor in salvation. He was religious, but he did not know the reality of redemption.

Paul reminds us in Romans 8:35-39 that nothing should separate us from the love of God. Yet the reality is that many people allow possessions, ambitions, or relationships to stand between them and Christ. When we cling to anything more tightly than we cling to God, that thing becomes an idol. Jesus made it clear: if eternal life is the goal, we must be willing to let go of everything that keeps us from Him.

Take Up the Cross and Follow Jesus

Finally, Jesus told the man to take up the cross and follow Him. To take up the cross means more than carrying a burden. It means dying to self. It is the daily act of denying our fleshly desires and surrendering to God's will. Luke 9:23 records Jesus' words: "Whoever wants to be my disciple must deny themselves and take up their cross daily and follow me." Following Christ is not about adding Him to our lives while keeping everything else as it is. It is about surrendering fully, leaving behind what pleases the flesh, and living for Him.

The rich young ruler heard the call but walked away sorrowful because he was unwilling to make the sacrifice. He left with his wealth intact but with his soul still in jeopardy. He gained temporary comfort but missed eternal life. His story is a tragic reminder that salvation requires surrender. We cannot hold on to the world and take hold of Christ at the same time.

Final Word

Prioritizing wealth, status, or possessions over Jesus leads to shallow faith and a distorted view of life. It robs us of the eternal riches that can only be found in Christ. True fulfillment comes not from clinging to the temporary but from surrendering to the eternal. Eternal life is a gift, but it requires us to yield everything to the One who gave everything for us.

The question of the rich young ruler is the question every person must ask: What must I do to inherit eternal life? The answer is clear. Know God's truth. Separate yourself from anything that stands between you and Him. Take up your cross, deny yourself, and follow Jesus. That is the only path to true life now and forever.

Lesson 8
How to Handle Evil Doers

Scripture: Psalms 37

The Struggle of Living Among the Wicked

Psalm 37 is a practical guide for navigating life in a world where evil people often appear to prosper while the righteous face difficulty. Within this psalm, David offers wisdom to find joy, resist bitterness, and keep a godly perspective in the face of injustice. The psalm is filled with warnings about what not to do as well as guidance on how we should respond when we see ungodly people succeed and godly people suffer. David speaks directly to our natural temptation to envy, to retaliate, and to allow anger to consume us. Instead of responding in such ways, Psalm 37 shows us how to trust God's timing and justice.

Principle One: Fret Not

Three times in this psalm, David instructs the reader to "fret not" (verses 1, 7, and 8). The Hebrew word for fret carries the idea of burning with anger. David warns us not to let the success of the wicked provoke us into jealousy or rage. When we allow resentment to take root, it leads to spiritual damage and ungodly behavior. Evil doers may seem to prosper for a season, but their judgment will surely come.

Instead of envying their gain or letting their actions get under our skin, we are called to keep our hearts free from bitterness. If we allow anger to dominate us, we risk speaking or acting in ways that dishonor God. Psalm 37:23 reminds us that "the steps of a good man are ordered by the Lord." Rather than letting the behavior of others dictate our response, we are to remain steady in the assurance that God is guiding our path. To fret is to give the enemy control of our emotions. To trust God is to rest in His sovereignty and to remember that justice belongs to Him.

Principle Two: Trust God

In verse 3, David directs us to "trust in the Lord." Trusting God is not a slogan or a cliché. It is an intentional act of reliance on His care and provision. Trust means leaning on God when life feels unfair, choosing to believe that He sees our struggle and will act in His time. Trusting God means humbling ourselves, casting every burden onto Him, and resting in the promise that He will sustain us.

Jesus Himself affirmed this truth when He reminded His followers not to worry about what they would eat, drink, or wear, for the God who provides for the birds of the air and the lilies of the field will also provide for His children (Matthew 6:31-34). To trust God is to believe He has our lives in His hands even when our circumstances do not make sense. The ungodly may appear to be winning, but those who trust the Lord will see His justice prevail.

Principle Three: Do Good

In verses 27–29, David teaches us that the way to respond to evil is not with retaliation but with goodness. When people mistreat us, the human response is to strike back. Yet David counsels us to focus instead on pleasing God through doing good. This principle echoes throughout Scripture. James 4:17 reminds us that if we know the good, we ought to do and fail to do it, we sin. Galatians teaches that when we do good, we will reap the harvest of what we have sown. Romans 12:19-21 instructs us to overcome evil with good rather than being overcome by evil ourselves.

Doing good does not mean we are blind to wrongdoing or indifferent to injustice. It means that our response reflects God's character rather than our anger. Evil will not be defeated by more evil. Only goodness rooted in God's love has the power to break the cycle of hatred and bring glory to His name.

Final Word: God Is in Control

Psalm 37 reminds us that God is the Architect and Director of our lives. He sees the schemes of the wicked, and He knows the struggles of the righteous. When we fret, we lose focus on His sovereignty. When we retaliate, we step outside of His will. But when we trust Him, do good, and keep our eyes fixed on Him, we experience peace even in the presence of evil.

Your life is not in the hands of your enemies. It is in the hands of God. He is faithful to care for you and to bring justice in His time. Therefore, resist the temptation to burn with anger. Choose instead to trust, to do good, and to walk in the confidence that the Lord is guiding your steps.

Lesson 9
Spiritual Maturity

Scripture: Acts 4:23-33

Defining Spiritual Maturity

Spiritual maturity is the process of continual growth in one's faith and relationship with God. It is not tied to a particular age or stage of life, but rather it is an ongoing journey of learning to live in a way that reflects God's character. A spiritually mature believer strives to live according to God's will and commandments instead of being guided solely by personal opinions or desires. Maturity in faith involves acknowledging our limitations and depending on God's grace. This posture of humility allows others to see Christ's love through us.

Spiritual maturity is also marked by perseverance. It means facing trials and difficulties with a heart anchored in God's faithfulness. Instead of giving up when life becomes difficult, the mature Christian endures with trust in God, drawing strength from Him to keep moving forward. This kind of maturity produces wisdom, humility, and the ability to respond with grace in every season of life.

The Example of the Early Church

The fourth chapter of Acts provides a portrait of a spiritually mature church. Verses 23–33 highlight the way the early Christians responded to persecution. After Peter and John were arrested and threatened by the religious leaders for preaching in the name of Jesus, they were released and returned to their fellow believers. Rather than responding in fear or anger, the church gathered together in prayer. They shared in unity, sought God's presence, and received a fresh outpouring of the Holy Spirit. Scripture records that after they prayed, the place where they were assembled was shaken, and they were all filled with the Holy Spirit. With renewed strength, they continued to proclaim the word of God with boldness.

This passage reveals an important truth. The church cannot grow in numbers without first maturing in spirit. Spiritual maturity is not simply about professing faith in Christ. It is about deepening that faith, growing in His likeness, and living out His truth in every circumstance.

Prayer: The Foundation of Growth

Acts 4 reminds us that prayer is central to spiritual maturity. When persecution and trials arose, the early believers turned to prayer. They did not rely on their own strength or strategies but lifted their voices together to God. Their unity in prayer invited God's power, and as a result, the Holy Spirit filled them and gave them courage to stand firm.

This example teaches us that followers of Christ cannot grow without prayer. A mature Christian life is cultivated in the presence of God. It is through consistent prayer that believers gain strength, wisdom, and resilience. When challenges come, prayer grounds us in God's promises and aligns us with His will.

The Role of the Holy Spirit

The early believers also matured through the indwelling of the Holy Spirit. Acts 4:31 describes how they were filled with the Spirit, and this filling equipped them with boldness and clarity in their witness. The Spirit gave them courage to speak the truth and wisdom to navigate opposition.

No believer can truly mature in Christ without the Holy Spirit. It is the Spirit who teaches, convicts, empowers, and comforts us. Without His presence, our growth remains shallow and incomplete. With His presence, we are transformed into people who reflect the character of Christ.

The Grace of God

Another key element in spiritual maturity seen in Acts 4:33 is grace. The early believers were able to grow because of the favor of God resting upon them. Grace sustained them, strengthened them, and enabled them to live daily in God's will. Their maturity was not the result of human effort alone but of divine empowerment.

Grace remains the foundation of growth for every Christian today. We are saved because of God's grace, and we are called to continue maturing in that same grace. Spiritual maturity means living with a constant awareness that every blessing, every opportunity, and every step forward comes from the unearned favor of God. His grace not only saves us but also carries us as we grow in faith.

Final Word: The Call to Keep Growing

Spiritual maturity is not a destination we arrive at and remain. It is a continual process of growth in knowledge, faith, and obedience. The example of the early church reminds us that prayer, the Holy Spirit, and God's grace are essential to this journey. Christians are not meant to plateau in their faith or settle for spiritual complacency. We are called to keep pressing forward, deepening our understanding of God, and reflecting His character more fully in our lives.

The church today, just like the early believers, must be willing to pray earnestly, depend on the Spirit, and rely on grace. As we do, we will not only endure trials with strength but also shine with boldness as witnesses of Christ. Spiritual maturity is the fruit of a life rooted in God, continually growing toward His purpose and glory.

Lesson 10
Three Benefits for the Child of God

Scripture: Psalm 103:1-4

The Call to Worship and Remember

Psalm 103 is a hymn of praise and thanksgiving, a psalm Israel sang in celebration of God's goodness and compassion. Worship was central to their faith, and David calls the people to bless the Lord with all that is within them. Whenever we gather in worship, this psalm reminds us that we, too, must lift our voices to celebrate God's mercy. The late gospel singer Ethel Waters captured this spirit of praise when she sang at a Billy Graham crusade, "I sing because I'm happy. I sing because I'm free. His eye is on the sparrow, and I know He watches me." Worship is more than a song. It is a declaration that God is good, merciful, and faithful to His children.

One of the great challenges believers face is what might be called "identity amnesia." This is when we forget who God is and who we are as His children. Such forgetfulness leaves us spiritually weak and vulnerable to fear, anxiety, and discouragement. When we lose sight of our identity in Christ, we also forget the blessings and benefits that are uniquely ours as children of God. David warns us against this forgetfulness, saying in Psalm 103:2, "Bless the Lord, O my soul, and forget not all his benefits." In Psalm 116:12, he also asks, "What shall I render to the Lord for all his benefits toward me?" Forgetfulness robs us of joy and leaves us ungrateful for the blessings we have already received.

Paul in Philippians 3:13 also reminds believers that while we are not to forget the benefits of God, there are things from our past that we should leave behind. He says, "Forgetting those things which are behind, and reaching forth unto those things which are before." We cannot change the past, but we can choose how we respond to it. Dwelling on old mistakes or hurts does not change them, but remembering God's mercy and moving forward in His grace transforms our future.

In Psalm 103, David highlights three key benefits for every child of God: forgiveness, healing, and redemption.

The Benefit of Forgiveness

The first benefit David names is forgiveness. Psalm 103:3 declares that God forgives all our sins. Forgiveness is not earned but granted by a merciful God who cleanses us when we confess and repent. First John 1:9 affirms that if we confess our sins, He is faithful and just to forgive us and cleanse us from all unrighteousness. David himself knew the crushing weight of guilt. In Psalm 51, he pleaded with God to wash him, cleanse him, and create in him a clean heart. God responded with mercy.

The ministry of Jesus also revealed this benefit. In Luke 5:20, Jesus forgave the sins of the paralyzed man before healing his body. In Luke 7:37-48, He forgave the sinful woman who washed His feet with her tears and wiped them with her hair. Forgiveness is not limited to a select few. It is extended to all who come to God in faith. For every believer, forgiveness is the foundation of our relationship with God and the assurance that our sins no longer define us.

The Benefit of Healing

The second benefit David acknowledges is healing. Psalm 103:3 continues by declaring that God heals all diseases. The God who created us from the dust of the ground (Genesis 2:7) is more than able to restore what is broken. Throughout Scripture, God demonstrates His power to heal. He healed Naaman of leprosy when he obeyed the prophet's instructions to wash in the Jordan River (2 Kings 5:10–14). He healed King Hezekiah, who had been told he would die, and added fifteen years to his life (Isaiah 38:1–5). In the New Testament, Jesus healed the woman who had suffered from bleeding for twelve years (Mark 5:25–34) and Peter healed the lame man at the temple gate through the power of Christ (Acts 3:1–8).

The testimony of God's healing power continues today. Many believers can recall moments when God's hand brought physical, emotional, or spiritual healing. Some healings are immediate, others come through a process, and still others will be completed in eternity. But the truth remains: the God who heals is still at work. Healing is His gift to His children and a benefit of belonging to Him.

The Benefit of Redemption

The third benefit David describes is redemption. In Psalm 103:4, he declares that God redeems our life from destruction. David himself experienced God's deliverance many times when his life was on the line. Redemption means being bought back, rescued from bondage, and restored to freedom. Ultimately, God's greatest act of redemption was sending His Son, Jesus Christ. John 3:16 tells us that God gave His only begotten Son so that whoever believes in Him will not perish but have everlasting life. Redemption is not only about being saved from sin's penalty but also about being delivered from sin's power.

Romans 8:34 reminds us that Christ not only died and rose again but also now intercedes for us. He stands as our advocate, ensuring that redemption is not just a moment in time but a continuing reality. Every believer can live with the assurance that we are redeemed, restored, and reconciled to God.

Final Word: The Fullness of God's Benefits

David concludes Psalm 103 by pointing to the fullness of God's benefits. In verse 5, he writes that God satisfies our desires with good things. In Psalm 107:8-9, he reaffirms that it is God who fills the hungry soul with goodness. Isaiah 40:29–31 declares that God gives strength to the weary and power to the weak, renewing the strength of those who wait on Him.

The benefits of God are not small or temporary. They are eternal gifts that sustain, heal, and redeem us. Forgiveness restores our relationship with Him. Healing mends what is broken. Redemption secures our place in His family forever. As children of God, we must not forget these benefits but live daily in gratitude for them.

Lift your voice like David and bless the Lord with all that is within you. Remember His forgiveness, trust His healing, and rejoice in His redemption. These are the benefits that belong to every child of God.

Lesson 11
Commit to God, Family, and Church

Selective Scriptures

Understanding Commitment and Priority

Priority is what or who we value most. Before a person can truly commit themselves to anyone or anything, they must honestly answer a few important questions. Who is the most important person in your life? What is the most important thing in your life? What do you enjoy doing more than anything else? The way we answer these questions reveals what we truly prioritize.

Both Christians and non-Christians struggle in this area. Many do not know who or what should be their first priority. Some give first place to themselves, others to work, hobbies, or even relationships. But the Word of God is clear. There is a divine order for our commitments. If we desire to live according to God's will, our commitments must first be directed to Him, then to our families, and then to the church.

Commit to God First

Jesus teaches us in Matthew 6:33 to "seek first the kingdom of God and his righteousness, and all these things shall be added unto you." God is not to be placed second to relatives, friends, work, or activities. He is to be our first and greatest priority. Jesus further says in Matthew 10:37–40 that anyone who loves family or possessions more than Him is not worthy of Him.

Being committed to God means placing Him before everything and everyone else, including ourselves. Luke 9:23 makes this clear: "If anyone would come after me, he must deny himself and take up his cross daily and follow me." Commitment to God also requires loving Him with all of our heart, soul, mind, and strength (Mark 12:30). This commitment is not part-time or reserved for Sunday mornings. God desires to be first in our lives every moment of every day.

Commit to Family Second

After God, our next priority should be our families. From the beginning of creation, God established the family as the first human institution (Genesis 1:27; 2:7; 2:21–25; 4:1–2). Family is a gift from God and must not be neglected. Too often, marriages and homes are destroyed because one or both spouses place other priorities, such as work, friends, or personal pursuits, before their commitment to family. Studies confirm this truth, with a significant percentage of divorces being attributed to a lack of commitment.

Scripture strongly warns against neglecting family responsibilities. First Timothy 5:8 teaches that anyone who fails to provide for their household denies the faith and is worse than an unbeliever. Husbands and wives are commanded in Ephesians 5:21–33 to love and submit to one another, not to give their attention to outside distractions or relationships. Parents also bear the responsibility of training their children in the ways of the Lord. Proverbs 22:6 reminds us to "train up a child in the way he should go, and when he is old, he will not depart from it." Family commitment is a sacred duty that reflects our obedience to God.

Commit to the Church Third

Finally, commitment must extend to the church. Jesus declared in Matthew 16:18 that He would build His church and that the gates of hell would not prevail against it. Every believer who has been born again is called to commit to the church. The church is not simply a building; it is the body of Christ, the gathering place where believers come together to worship, to praise, and to grow in the Word of God.

The psalmist calls us to worship, saying, "Come, let us bow down in worship, let us kneel before the Lord our Maker" (Psalm 95:6). Psalm 100 and Psalm 150 both invite the people of God to praise Him with gladness and with music. Ephesians 5:27 assures us that when Christ returns, the church will be presented to Him without spot or wrinkle. This vision of a holy and radiant church should inspire us to commit wholeheartedly to its mission.

The church is also where we are spiritually nourished. First Peter 2:2 describes believers as newborn infants who crave pure spiritual milk so that they may grow in salvation. It is in the church that we are fed with the Word of God, equipped for service, and strengthened in faith. The church is also the place of fellowship, where we encourage one another in love and good works. Hebrews 10:25 reminds us not to neglect meeting together but to exhort one another.

Final Word: A Life of Ordered Commitment

When our commitments are properly ordered, our lives reflect God's will. God must come first, for He is the source of life and the foundation of every blessing. Family comes next, for God designed the home to be a place of love, nurture, and faithfulness. The church follows, as it is the institution God established to equip and empower His people for ministry.

The church is where believers are trained, built up, and given opportunities to use their gifts in service to God and others. A life committed to God, family, and church is a life that is balanced, fruitful, and pleasing to Him. When we align our priorities in this way, we find that everything else falls into its proper place.

Lesson 12
Three Reasons Why Christians Celebrate Pentecost

Scripture: Acts 2:1 thru 4

The Meaning of Pentecost

The word Pentecost means fiftieth. It is observed on the fiftieth day after Easter, making it one of the great holy days of the Christian calendar. Historically, Pentecost was associated with the Feast of First Fruits, when God's people would offer back to Him the first part of their harvest or the firstborn of their flocks (Exodus 22:29; Deuteronomy 26:2–4; Genesis 4:3–4). These offerings were acts of worship, expressing gratitude to God and trust in His continued provision. Proverbs 3:9 and Malachi 3:10 emphasize the importance of honoring God with our first fruits, reminding us that everything we have comes from Him.

For Christians, Pentecost takes on a deeper spiritual meaning. It reminds us not only of God's provision but also of His promises yet to come. It is a day of thanksgiving for blessings already received and a celebration of the blessings that await us. Pentecost is also a day of unity, when people of many languages heard the Apostles' message and understood it, symbolizing that in Christ all believers are one family.

In Acts 2, we see three powerful reasons why Christians celebrate Pentecost: the coming of the Holy Spirit, the birth of the church, and the reminder of God's providential care.

The Coming of the Holy Spirit

The first reason Christians celebrate Pentecost is that it marks the day the Holy Spirit came to dwell within believers. In Acts 1, Jesus had instructed His disciples to wait in Jerusalem for the promised gift of the Holy Spirit (Acts 1:1–5). In Acts 2:1–4, while the Apostles and other believers were gathered together in prayer, they suddenly heard a sound like a mighty rushing wind. Tongues that appeared as fire rested on each of them, and they were all filled with the Holy Spirit. They began to speak in other tongues as the Spirit enabled them.

This moment fulfilled the promise of Christ and marked a new era for the people of God. The Holy Spirit empowered the believers to carry out the mission of Christ with boldness, wisdom, and strength. Pentecost is celebrated because it was the day when God's Spirit no longer dwelt only in temples made by hands but came to live in the hearts of His people.

The Birth of the Church

The second reason Christians celebrate Pentecost is that it marks the birth of the church. In Matthew 16:13–18, Jesus told Peter that He would build His church and that the gates of hell would not prevail against it. This promise was realized at Pentecost when the Spirit descended, and the church was born in power. The believers who had once been fearful and uncertain were now filled with courage, boldly proclaiming the gospel of Jesus Christ.

The church has endured for centuries not because the devil has refrained from attacking it, but because Christ promised that the devil would not overcome it. Isaiah 54:17 assures us that "no weapon formed against you shall prosper." The very existence and endurance of the church testify to the faithfulness of God's promise. Pentecost is celebrated because it reminds us that the church is not a human invention, but a divine institution established by Christ Himself.

The Providential Care of God

The third reason Christians celebrate Pentecost is that it reminds us of God's providential care. God's care is His protective hand over those who belong to Him. Deuteronomy 20:4 reminds us that the Lord goes with His people to fight for them and give them victory. Psalm 121:5–8 proclaims that the Lord watches over us, protecting our coming and going both now and forever. Second Corinthians 4:8–9 shows us that although we may be hard pressed, perplexed, or struck down, we are never abandoned by God.

The Bible offers many examples of God's protective care. In Genesis 7, He preserved Noah and his family during the flood. In Exodus 14:21–31, He protected Moses and the Israelites from Pharaoh and his army by parting the Red Sea. In Mark 4:35-41, Jesus calmed a storm and protected His disciples from danger. These accounts remind us that the God who acted in the past is the same God who protects us today. Pentecost celebrates this ongoing care, for the Spirit's presence within us is also the assurance of God's daily protection.

Final Word: A Day of Celebration and Assurance

We celebrate Pentecost because it is the day God poured out His Spirit on all believers, the day the church was born, and the day we are reminded that God's care surrounds us at all times. The Spirit empowers us, the church unites us, and God's protection sustains us. Pentecost is not just a historical event but a living reality. Each time we celebrate it, we declare that the same God who moved in Jerusalem on that fiftieth day after Easter is still moving in our lives today.

The God we serve is protecting us every day. Pentecost is our reminder that He is present, He is faithful, and He is with us always.

Lesson 13
Surrender Your Body, Mind (Heart), and Soul to God

Scripture: Romans 12:1-2

The Battle for Your Life

The enemy's agenda is to use ungodly, worldly, and fleshly influences to weaken your relationship with Christ and separate you from the love of God. Yet Paul reminds us in Romans 8:35–39 that nothing has the power to separate true believers from God's love in Christ Jesus. This is why Christianity teaches us to resist the devil and find satisfaction in Christ alone (James 4:7; Matthew 16:26; Psalm 107:8–9).

In today's world, it is easy for Christians to fall into a mindset of selfishness and shallow pursuits. A desire for wealth, comfort, and recognition consumes many. But the Word of God calls us to a different mindset. Philippians 2:5 exhorts us to have the same mind as Christ, one of humility and obedience. Romans 12:2 further calls us to reject conformity to the world and instead be transformed by the renewing of our minds. Spiritual transformation is not about following the world's patterns but about surrendering every part of ourselves to God.

In Romans 12:1–2, Paul lays out what it means to fully yield to God. To live a life that pleases Him, we must surrender our bodies, our minds, and our souls.

Three Things You Must Surrender to God

I. Your Body (v.1)

Paul begins in Romans 12:1 by urging believers to present their bodies as living sacrifices, holy and acceptable to God. The human body has been corrupted by sin. From the moment Adam disobeyed God in the Garden of Eden, sin entered the world, bringing condemnation upon all humanity (Romans 5:12). As Paul later wrote, all have sinned and fall short of the glory of God (Romans 3:23).

When we are saved, we are not only forgiven but also called to surrender our bodies to God for His purposes. Our bodies are not our own. First Corinthians 3:16–17 and 6:19 remind us that our bodies are temples of the Holy Spirit. The Spirit of God lives within us, making our bodies sacred vessels for His glory. To surrender our bodies means to honor God with how we live, what we do, and how we use the physical strength and life He has given us. It is not about perfection, but about dedicating ourselves daily to His service.

II. Your Mind (v. 2a)

In Romans 12:2, Paul turns our attention to the mind. He warns that the world seeks to control how we think, but God desires to transform our minds. The enemy often attacks through the mind by planting seeds of doubt, pride, or temptation. Once these seeds take root, they can lead to sinful desires and actions. This is why Proverbs 4:23 warns us to guard our hearts, for everything we do flows from them. Proverbs 23:7 further emphasizes that as a person thinks in their heart, so are they.

60

To remain in God's will, we must yield our minds to Him. Peter instructs believers in 1 Peter 1:13 to prepare our minds for action and be sober-minded, setting our hope fully on God's grace. In 1 Peter 5:8–9, he adds that we must be alert and resist the devil, who prowls like a roaring lion seeking to devour. Surrendering the mind to God means allowing Him to reshape our thoughts, desires, and perspectives. It is a commitment to think with clarity, to meditate on His Word, and to resist the lies of the enemy.

III. Our Soul (v. 2b)

Finally, Paul speaks to the surrender of the soul. Humanity is triune, consisting of body, mind, and soul. Yielding one part without the others creates imbalance and instability. James 1:8 warns that a double-minded person is unstable in all their ways. To surrender the soul is to yield the very essence of who we are, our will, our emotions, and our eternal being to God.

This surrender is not a one-time act but an ongoing process. It begins the moment we are born again and continues throughout our walk with Christ. Second Peter 3:18 reminds us to grow in the grace and knowledge of our Lord and Savior Jesus Christ. Spiritual maturity requires continually yielding our whole selves to God, allowing Him to shape us daily until He calls us home or until Christ returns.

Final Word: Living Fully Surrendered

Paul's call in Romans 12:1–2 is clear. A life surrendered to God involves more than words or good intentions. It requires the daily presentation of our bodies as living sacrifices, the ongoing renewal of our minds, and the wholehearted yielding of our souls. The world seeks to draw us away, but God calls us to transformation.

When we give ourselves entirely to Him, we experience true freedom. Our bodies become instruments of righteousness, our minds are renewed with truth, and our souls are anchored in His grace. This is the path of a surrendered life, and it is the only way to live in the fullness of God's purpose.

Lesson 14
Three Lessons from Bees

Scripture: Judges 14:8

Sub-Theme: Learn How to Thrive in Life

The Difference Between Surviving and Thriving

To thrive in life, we can learn from the example of bees. Life on earth teaches us that there is a difference between merely surviving and truly thriving. To survive is to endure hardship and make it through affliction, adversity, and misery. Each of us has faced seasons of turmoil, whether through trials, sickness, financial strain, or spiritual exhaustion. Yet we can testify that we are survivors because God has brought us through. First Chronicles 16:11 calls us to seek the Lord and His strength, and 2 Corinthians 4:8–9 reminds us that even when pressed on every side, we are not crushed, because God sustains us.

Survival is a blessing, but God desires that we go beyond survival and flourish. The hymn writer expressed this beautifully in "Amazing Grace" when he wrote, "'Tis grace hath brought me safe thus far, and grace will lead me home." Third John 1:2 tells us that God desires His children to prosper and be in health. Believers are called not just to get by but to bloom, like a rose that blossoms and displays its beauty. Thriving means living a fruitful, prosperous, and blessed life that brings glory to God.

What It Means to Thrive

To thrive is to prosper, to flourish, and to succeed in what God has called us to do. It is to live with joy and abundance, walking in the blessings that come from obedience and faith. Thriving is not simply about material wealth. It is about living a life that reflects God's favor, peace, and purpose. God has not called us to lives of mediocrity or just enough. He desires that we live abundantly, thriving in every area of our walk with Him.

Lesson One: Create a Royal Buzz

The first lesson we learn from bees is the importance of creating a sound that brings life. The buzzing of bees serves a purpose. When certain species of buzz-pollinating bees visit a flower, the vibrations of their wings and bodies release the pollen, allowing it to be carried and deposited on the next flower. This process causes plants to bloom and produce fruit.

Our lives also create a sound. The question is, what kind of sound are we producing? Are our words creating peace or chaos? Do we spread joy or anger, healing or hurt? Are our conversations filled with encouragement, or do we constantly nag, complain, or tear others down with bitterness and hate? Like the bee's buzz, our words have the power to pollinate the lives of others, causing them to grow and flourish. Ephesians 4:29 tells us to use words that build others up according to their needs. Jesus Himself emphasized love as the foundation of our witness when He said in John 13:34–35 and John 15:11–12 that we are to love one another as He has loved us.

Our words frame the atmosphere around us. When we speak with grace, encouragement, and love, we contribute to the growth of those around us. Thriving begins when our "buzz" brings life.

Lesson Two: Respect Leadership

The second lesson we learn from bees is the importance of respecting leadership. In a beehive, the queen bee holds a vital role. She is respected by the other bees because of her position, and her responsibility is to provide order and continuity within the hive. The success of the hive depends on the respect and structure maintained around her role.

Similarly, God has ordained leadership in both the secular and spiritual realms. Romans 13:1–2 instructs us to submit to governing authorities, acknowledging that all authority comes from God. Hebrews 13:17 calls believers to obey their leaders and submit to them, recognizing that they watch over our souls. First Thessalonians 5:12–13 reminds us to acknowledge and respect those who labor among us and provide spiritual guidance.

To thrive in life and in faith, we must learn to respect leadership. It is impossible to obey someone you do not honor. Respect for leaders in the home, the workplace, the community, and the church brings order, unity, and blessing. Disrespect, on the other hand, breeds disorder and hinders growth. Thriving requires a spirit of humility that honors the authority God has placed in our lives.

Lesson Three: Work as a Team

The third lesson from bees is the power of teamwork. Bees function as a colony, with each bee playing a vital role. Their survival and productivity depend on their ability to work together. No single bee can accomplish the work of the hive alone.

In the same way, the body of Christ functions as a team. First Corinthians 12:12 teaches that though the body is made up of many members, it is still one body. Each believer has a gift, and together these gifts build the church and strengthen the mission. First Corinthians 14:40 further reminds us that everything must be done in a fitting and orderly way. When believers work together, respecting each other's roles and supporting each other's gifts, the church thrives.

Better things are always accomplished when we work as a team. Teamwork allows us to combine strengths, cover weaknesses, and move forward with greater effectiveness. Thriving in life and ministry requires collaboration, unity, and mutual support.

Final Word: Thriving in Unity

Bees teach us that life is not only about survival but about thriving. To thrive, we must create a sound that brings life, respect the leadership God has placed over us, and work together as a team. Ecclesiastes 4:9–10 reminds us that two are better than one, for if one falls, the other can help them up. Psalm 133:1–3 declares how good and pleasant it is when God's people live together in unity.

There should be no divisions or discord within the body of Christ. Leaders and members alike are called to work together for the cause of Jesus Christ. Thriving in life means living in unity, flourishing in our gifts, and building one another up in love. Like the bees, may we learn to live with purpose, order, and teamwork, bringing glory to God in all that we do.

Lesson 15
A Charge to Keep

Scripture: II Timothy 1:8-10

Paul's Context and Message

To study the books of 1 and 2 Timothy is to step into the final season of the Apostle Paul's ministry. At the time of this writing, Paul was imprisoned in Rome, awaiting execution. He had been accused, arrested, tried, and found guilty. Many had abandoned him, and now, with his life nearing its end, Paul wrote with urgency and passion to his son in the ministry, Timothy. His words were both personal and pastoral, meant to encourage Timothy to remain loyal to his calling and faithful in ministry.

The book of 2 Timothy stands out in several ways. It is Paul's last will and testament, his final letter before his death. It belongs to the group of writings known as the Pastoral Epistles, which include 1 Timothy, 2 Timothy, and Titus. Unlike Paul's letters to churches, this epistle was personal, addressed directly to Timothy, his young disciple. Yet within its pages, Paul also provides ecclesiastical guidance, answering questions about order and organization in the church. Furthermore, it serves as an apologetic work, defending the Christian faith against false teachings such as Gnosticism that threatened the church of that time.

In 2 Timothy, Paul delivers a series of charges, not only to Timothy but to every believer in Christ. These charges remind us of our responsibility to guard what God has entrusted to us faithfully.

Charge One: Keep Your Spiritual Gifts Blazing

The first charge Paul gives Timothy is to keep his spiritual gifts alive and active. In 2 Timothy 1:6, Paul urges him to "stir up the gift of God" that was within him. The imagery is that of a fire that must be fanned into flame, continually tended so it does not die out. Timothy had been equipped with gifts for ministry, and Paul wanted him to use those gifts boldly and faithfully.

This same charge applies to all church leaders and believers today. God has placed within each of us spiritual gifts meant to serve His kingdom. These gifts are not to be neglected or hidden but kept alive, blazing, and active. It is our responsibility to exercise these gifts for the glory of God and the building up of the church. Gifts unused eventually grow cold, but gifts stirred and activated grow stronger. Paul's words remind us that thriving ministry requires intentional effort to keep the fire of our calling burning brightly.

Charge Two: Hold Fast to Jesus

The second charge Paul gives is to hold fast to Christ. In 2 Timothy 1:13–14, he tells Timothy to "hold fast the pattern of sound words" and to guard the truth entrusted to him through the Holy Spirit. To hold fast means to cling tightly, refusing to let go. It is to maintain a firm grip even when difficulties arise.

Paul knew that Timothy would face hardships and opposition, and so he urged him to remain steadfast. Holding fast is not passive. It is an act of determination and devotion. It is choosing to trust Christ when times are dark and when friends are few. It is clinging to the Word of God when false teachings surround us. Hymn writers captured this spirit in the call to "hold to God's unchanging hand." That is the essence of this charge.

For us today, holding fast means refusing to let trials shake our faith. It means trusting Jesus as the friend who never leaves us and the Savior who never fails. In every season, our grip must remain on Him.

Charge Three: Be Strong in the Grace of Christ

The third charge comes in 2 Timothy 2:1, where Paul tells Timothy, "Be strong in the grace that is in Christ Jesus." Strength here does not come from human willpower but from God's undeserved favor. Grace is God granting blessings we do not deserve, and Paul makes clear that this grace is what sustains both church leaders and ordinary believers.

To be strong in the Lord means to recognize that we cannot endure life's challenges in our own strength. It means leaning fully on Christ, who empowers us to stand firm when trials come. Being strong in grace means acknowledging our weakness and depending on His strength. It is a reminder that true power is not in independence but in complete reliance on the Lord Jesus Christ. Paul knew that Timothy would need this strength, and so do we.

Final Word: A Hymn of Commitment

Paul's charges remind us that the Christian life requires dedication, perseverance, and faith. They echo through history and remain relevant for us today. We, too, must keep our spiritual gifts blazing, hold fast to Christ, and be strong in His grace.

As I reflect on this charge, I remember my childhood in the First Baptist Church of Coolwell, Virginia, where my late pastor, J.P. Rose, would lead the congregation in an old hymn that captures the essence of this lesson:

"A charge to keep I have,
A God to glorify,
Who gave His Son my soul to save,
And fit it for the sky.

To serve this present age,
My calling to fulfill,
O may it all my power engage,
To do my Master's will.

Arm me with jealous care,
As in Thy sight to live,
And O Thy servant, Lord, prepare,
A strict account to give.

Help me to watch and pray,
And on Thyself rely,
By faith assured I will obey,
For I shall never die."

This hymn is more than words. It is a declaration of commitment. May we, like Timothy, accept the charges given to us and live lives that glorify God, serve this present age, and remain faithful until the end.

Lesson 16
To Believe in the Birth of Jesus

Scripture: Luke 2:13-14

The Four Gospel Portraits of Jesus

Reading the four Gospels, Matthew, Mark, Luke, and John, gives us a complete picture of the birth, life, and mission of Jesus Christ. Each writer presents Jesus from a unique perspective. Matthew presents Him as King (Matthew 2:1–2). As King, Jesus rules over both heaven and earth, possessing all authority and power. Mark presents Him as the Servant (Mark 10:42–45). As Servant, Jesus meets our needs and gives His life as the ultimate act of service. Luke presents Him as the Son of Man (Luke 19:10). As the Son of Man, Jesus entered humanity, born of a woman, and lived among us in the flesh. John presents Him as the Son of God (John 1:49; John 20:31). As the Son of God, Jesus is one with the Father, fully divine, holy, and without sin.

Luke's account in chapter 2 not only tells of the birth of the Savior of the world but also describes the angelic proclamation of good news to the shepherds (Luke 2:8–14). Luke emphasizes the humility of Christ's arrival, noting that there was no room for Him in the inn, so He was born in a stable and laid in a manger (Luke

2:7; Matthew 8:20). This simple yet profound beginning highlights both His humanity and His mission.

The question this raises for us is deeply personal: Do you have room in your heart for Jesus? Just as the inn had no space for Him, many lives are crowded with worldly pursuits, leaving little room for the Savior. Believing in the birth of Jesus means more than knowing the story. It means making room for Him in our hearts and lives.

Lesson One: To Believe in the Birth of Jesus Is to Praise Him

Luke 2 tells us that after the shepherds heard the angelic message and visited the stable in Bethlehem, they left rejoicing. They praised God for what they had seen and heard, confirming that everything happened just as the angels had told them (Luke 2:20). Their response was immediate praise.

This example reminds us that if we have experienced the saving power of Jesus Christ, we are obligated to praise Him. Praise is not optional; it is the natural response of a grateful heart. To believe in the birth of Jesus is to recognize that God has entered into our broken world with the gift of salvation, and that realization should move us to worship. When Christ is born in our hearts, our lips and lives should reflect continual praise to His name.

Lesson Two: To Believe in the Birth of Jesus Is to Receive Good News

Luke 2 also highlights the announcement of the angels, who declared to the shepherds that the birth of Jesus was good news of great joy for all people (Luke 2:10). The message of Christ's birth was not one of fear but of hope. It was the proclamation that God had sent His Son into the world to save and deliver His people from sin.

To believe in the birth of Jesus is to embrace this good news for ourselves. It is to understand that in Christ we know the omniscient God, who knows all things; the omnipotent Lord, who holds all power; and the omnipresent Savior, who is always with us. The birth of Jesus is the fulfillment of God's love for the world, sending His only begotten Son so that we might have eternal life. This is good news indeed, and it is news worth celebrating with joy.

Lesson Three: To Believe in the Birth of Jesus Is to Join the Angelic Song

The birth of Christ was not a quiet or hidden event in heaven's eyes. At the moment of His arrival, the angels burst forth in praise, declaring, "Glory to God in the highest, and on earth peace, goodwill toward men" (Luke 2:14). The angelic host recognized that the birth of Jesus was the ultimate display of God's glory and the greatest gift of peace to mankind.

Believing in the birth of Jesus means joining in that chorus of praise. It is lifting our voices in worship and declaring God's glory, not only in song but in how we live our lives. The message of the angels is still true today: Christ's coming brings peace to troubled hearts and offers goodwill to a broken world. We honor the birth of Jesus when we echo that heavenly praise with our words and actions.

Final Word: Make Room for the Savior

The birth of Jesus is not just a story to be retold at Christmas. It is the foundation of our faith and the turning point of human history. To believe in His birth is to praise Him, to embrace the good news of salvation, and to join the angelic host in glorifying God.

The question remains: do you have space in your heart for Him? Just as there was no room in the inn, many hearts remain crowded with distractions. Yet those who make room for Jesus experience the fullness of His peace and joy. Let us believe in His birth, not as history alone, but as a present reality that transforms our lives today.

Lesson 17
God Answers Prayers

Scripture: Isaiah 38:1 thru 7

The God Who Hears and Responds

To study the Bible is to discover the nature of God. Theology, the study of God, reveals His attributes. Scripture teaches us that He is omnipresent, present everywhere at the same time (Psalm 139:7–10; Jeremiah 23:23–24). He is omniscient, knowing all things (1 John 3:20; Psalm 147:5). He is omnipotent, holding all power and authority (Matthew 28:18; Revelation 19:5–6). He is immutable, never changing in His character or promises (Malachi 3:6; Isaiah 40:8). These truths are foundational, but this lesson focuses on another equally important truth. Beyond being everywhere, all-knowing, all-powerful, and unchanging, God is also the One who answers prayers.

Isaiah, whose name means "God is salvation," was called by God as a prophet in the year King Uzziah died (Isaiah 6:8–9). Uzziah had ruled Judah for 52 years, but his reign ended tragically when he was struck with leprosy for entering the temple and offering incense, something only priests were authorized to do. Isaiah himself was not without fault. He confessed that he was a man of unclean lips, surrounded by people of unclean speech. Yet God purified him, transforming him and commissioning him as His prophet (Isaiah 6:5–7).

This truth reminds us that God can use anyone for His purpose. We are wrong when we assume God cannot use certain people. He delights in transforming sinners into servants who carry out His will.

Prayer as Communication with God

The first lesson Isaiah 38 teaches is that prayer is communication with God. King Hezekiah became sick and was told by the prophet Isaiah to set his house in order because he would soon die. In response, Hezekiah turned away from the world around him and prayed. His heartfelt communication with God changed the course of his life, and God extended his years (Isaiah 38:1–5).

Prayer has always been the way God's people connect with Him. Daniel prayed three times a day, even when it meant facing the lions' den (Daniel 6:10). Hannah poured out her heart in prayer when she longed for a child (1 Samuel 1:10–11). Jabez prayed boldly for God to enlarge his territory, and God granted his request (1 Chronicles 4:9–10). Paul and Silas prayed and sang hymns while in prison, and God shook the prison with His power (Acts 16:25). Even Jesus prayed in the Garden of Gethsemane, seeking strength from the Father in His moment of deepest agony (Matthew 26:36–46).

Matthew 7:7 assures us that if we ask, we will receive; if we seek, we will find; if we knock, the door will be opened. Prayer is not empty words but a conversation with the God who hears and responds.

God Answers the Prayers of Those in Relationship with Him

The second lesson is that God answers the prayers of those who are in a relationship with Him. Moses had an intimate relationship with God, and when he interceded on behalf of Israel, God heard and responded (Exodus 33:12–23). In Acts 12, when Peter was imprisoned, the church gathered to pray fervently. Their prayers were heard, and Peter was miraculously released. Scripture records that he went to the very house where the believers were still gathered in prayer, and they were astonished to see God's answer so quickly fulfilled (Acts 12:5, 12–16).

These examples remind us that prayer is not a formula but a fruit of a relationship. God does not close His ears to those who walk with Him. Having a relationship with God is one of the keys to answered prayer. The more we know Him, the more we learn to pray according to His will, and the more we experience the joy of seeing Him respond.

God Answers the Prayers of the Faithful

The third lesson is that God answers the prayers of the faithful. Revelation 2:10 encourages believers to be faithful, even to the point of death, with the promise of eternal life. Faithfulness means loyalty to God, trustworthiness in our walk, and steadfastness in our commitment. It is more than saying we believe; it is living out that belief daily with consistency and perseverance.

To be faithful is to remain loyal to God when trials arise, to continue praying when answers seem delayed, and to trust Him when life feels uncertain. Faithful believers do not let circumstances shake their devotion. Instead, they hold fast to God's promises, believing that He will honor their prayers in His perfect time and way.

Final Word: God's Response Is Always Sure

The story of Hezekiah reminds us that God hears and answers prayers. Sometimes the answer is yes, sometimes it is no, and sometimes it is wait. Yet every answer is evidence that God is listening and responding in the way that is best for us. The good news is that whether the answer comes quickly or slowly, whether it is the outcome we hoped for or a redirection we did not expect, God is always faithful to answer.

Our responsibility is to remain prayerful, remain in relationship with Him, and remain faithful. When we do, we will see in our own lives what Isaiah 38 reveals: that God is the One who not only hears but also answers prayer.

Lesson 18
Lessons from Elijah
the Prophet

Scripture: I Kings 17:1-5; James 5:17-18

Elijah's Context and Ministry

Elijah the prophet entered the biblical story after the reigns of King David and King Solomon, during a time when Israel was divided into two kingdoms: Israel in the north and Judah in the south. The northern kingdom of Israel had turned away from God, embracing idol worship in violation of the commandments given in Exodus 20:3–5. Their disobedience brought them out of alignment with God, and Elijah was sent to confront their sin. In 1 Kings 17:1–5, Elijah declared to King Ahab that there would be no rain except at his word. He then obeyed God's command to hide by the brook Cherith, where the Lord sustained him with water from the brook and food delivered by ravens.

James 5:17–18 highlights Elijah's prayer life. James reminds us that Elijah, though a prophet, was human like us. He prayed earnestly, and the rain ceased for three and a half years. Then he prayed again, and the heavens gave rain, restoring fruit to the land. Elijah's story demonstrates the power of prayer and the importance of obedience to God's Word.

Elijah's life teaches us that idolatry separates people from God. Today, people may not bow before carved images, but many still worship modern idols such as materialism, greed, selfishness, racism, injustice, lust, dishonesty, hatefulness, and hypocrisy. These false gods hinder our relationship with the true and living God. Believers must guard against such distractions and, like Paul teaches in Romans 8:35–39, remain steadfast so that nothing separates us from the love of Christ. Elijah's testimony also reminds us that the company we should seek is not worldly approval or "ride-or-die" companions but the presence of Jesus Himself (Matthew 17:1–3; James 5:17–18).

Lesson One: Believers Are Not Exempt from Depression

One of the most powerful lessons from Elijah's life is that being a believer does not exempt us from depression. Elijah was a faithful prophet, a man of prayer, and a follower of God, yet when threatened by Jezebel, he became overwhelmed and afraid. In 1 Kings 19:3–4, Elijah fled into the wilderness, sat down under a broom tree, and prayed that he might die. He experienced deep despair, feeling worthless and hopeless, despite his close relationship with God.

This reminds us that depression is real. It can affect anyone, regardless of their faith or position. The attitudes and behaviors of those around us can contribute to our struggles, and even those strong in faith can feel the crushing weight of mental and emotional exhaustion. When depression comes, the solution is not to isolate ourselves. Instead, we should confide in people we trust, lean on our support systems, and, when necessary, seek professional help. Elijah's experience teaches us that acknowledging our struggles is not weakness. It is part of the journey to restoration.

Lesson Two: God Speaks in Stillness

Another lesson from Elijah is that God does not always answer prayers in dramatic or miraculous ways. When Elijah was hiding in despair, God called him to stand on the mountain. In 1 Kings 19:11–13, there was a powerful wind, an earthquake, and a fire, yet God was not in those dramatic events. Instead, He came in a gentle whisper. When Elijah heard it, he recognized God's presence and wrapped his face in his cloak, humbled before the Lord.

This reminds us that God often speaks in quietness rather than through spectacle. Sometimes we miss His voice because our lives are too busy or too noisy. Learning to slow down, to be still, and to listen allows us to hear the gentle guidance of God. Elijah's encounter shows us that God's power is not always displayed in outward force but in the inward peace and clarity of His presence.

Lesson Three: The Importance of Self-Care

A further lesson from Elijah's life is the importance of self-care. After Elijah prayed to die, God did not rebuke him. Instead, He provided rest, food, and water (1 Kings 19:1–8). Elijah slept, ate, and was strengthened for the journey ahead. This demonstrates that physical, mental, emotional, and spiritual well-being are all important in serving God effectively.

Self-care helps us avoid burnout, frustration, and exhaustion. Without it, we become overtired, irritable, and unable to fulfill our responsibilities. Self-care is not selfish; it is a way to recalibrate, to restore strength, and to reconnect with God and others. Elijah's restoration shows us that sometimes the first step in healing is simply to rest, to nourish ourselves, and to allow God's presence to refresh us.

Final Word: Embracing Wholeness

Elijah's life offers timeless lessons for every believer. His story reminds us that even the faithful can struggle with depression, but God's presence brings hope. It teaches us that God's voice often comes in stillness, not in noise or spectacle. And it affirms the value of self-care as a means of protecting our health and restoring our strength.

Third John 1:2 reflects God's desire for us: "Beloved, I pray that you may prosper in all things and be in health, just as your soul prospers." True wellness is holistic, involving the body, mind, and spirit. By learning from Elijah's journey, we are reminded to trust God through our struggles, to listen for His quiet voice, and to take intentional steps toward wholeness.

Lesson 19
Your Service to
The God of Your Salvation

Scripture: Romans 12:10 thru 15

The Purpose of Salvation

God created us and redeemed us for His purpose (Proverbs 16:4; Ephesians 2:10). Salvation is not only about being rescued from sin's penalty but also about being called into service for the living God. We were saved to glorify Him with our lives and to serve Him faithfully. Salvation frees us from the bondage of sin so that we might be active participants in God's work on earth.

This means that believers are not saved for themselves alone. We are saved to share the good news of God's grace, to be the hands and feet of Jesus in this world, and to show God's love through practical actions. First Peter 2:9 makes clear that God called us out of darkness so that we might proclaim His marvelous light to others. Jesus, before ascending to heaven, gave the Great Commission, instructing His followers to carry the gospel to all nations through teaching, preaching, and witnessing (Matthew 20:28; Mark 16:15; Acts 1:8).

Every Christian is called to service. Paul, in Galatians 5:13, teaches that the liberty given to us in Christ is not for selfish indulgence but for love expressed through serving one another. Service is the mark of spiritual maturity. While selfishness reflects immaturity, love is demonstrated through serving others and meeting their needs.

Presenting Yourself to the World

The first consideration for effective service is how you present yourself to the world. Romans 12:1 urges believers to present themselves as living sacrifices, holy and acceptable to God. This act of surrender is the foundation of Christian service. To serve God well, your life must reflect His character. The world should be able to see Christ in you.

When Jesus began His earthly ministry, He called Peter, Andrew, James, and John to follow Him, not to sit in places of honor, but to serve alongside Him. In the same way, Christians today are called not to seek recognition or glory but to humbly serve others in the name of Christ. Service begins with presenting yourself daily as a vessel available for God's use.

The Place to Serve

The second consideration is recognizing where service begins. God has given us a central place to serve: the local church. The church is not only a gathering place but also the hub of ministry and mission. James 1:22 reminds us to be doers of the Word, not hearers only. Service in the local church allows us to live out our faith through action.

The church is designed to be a lighthouse in the community, pointing people toward Christ (Matthew 5:14–16). Through its ministries, the church brings glory to God by meeting needs, proclaiming the gospel, and building up believers. Service to the God of our salvation is best expressed through faithful participation in the ministries of the local church, where believers work together to expand God's kingdom.

The Purpose of Service

The third consideration is understanding why we serve. God has a purpose for everything He does, and our purpose must align with His. As believers, our service has three primary purposes.

First, we serve to bring glory to God in everything we do (1 Corinthians 10:31). Service is not about our reputation but about God's honor. Second, we serve to build up and encourage one another. Jesus illustrated this in the parable of the Good Samaritan (Luke 10:30–37) and through His command to love one another (John 13:34–35). Service strengthens the body of Christ and demonstrates God's love in tangible ways. Third, we serve to carry the gospel to the unsaved so that they, too, may experience salvation (Acts 8:4-8). A service that does not include sharing the message of Christ is incomplete. God calls us to serve not only the church but also the world, bringing light into dark places.

The Power for Service

The fourth consideration is the source of our strength to serve. God, through Jesus Christ, has given every believer the power and authority to serve effectively. That power comes through the Holy Spirit. Jesus promised the Spirit would be our Helper and Teacher (John 14:26), and Paul affirms that the Spirit fills us with hope and strength (Romans 15:13).

Without the Spirit, our efforts would be weak and ineffective. With the Spirit, we are empowered to endure hardship, love difficult people, and carry out God's will. The Holy Spirit equips us with gifts for ministry and gives us the courage to use them for the benefit of others. Our service is not sustained by human strength but by divine empowerment.

Final Word: The Example of Jesus

In John 13:4–15, Jesus demonstrated the ultimate example of service by washing His disciples' feet. This humble act revealed that true greatness in the kingdom of God is found in serving others. He reminded His followers that if He, their Lord and Teacher, was willing to serve in such a way, then they too must serve one another.

Our service to the God of our salvation is not optional. It is the natural response of a life transformed by grace. Present yourself as a living sacrifice, serve faithfully in the local church, understand the purpose of your service, and rely on the Spirit for power. In doing so, you will honor God, strengthen others, and fulfill the calling placed upon your life.

Lesson 20
Faith In-spite Of

Scripture: Hebrews 11:1-7

The Power of Faith

The book of Hebrews, particularly chapter 11, offers one of the most straightforward and most inspiring explanations of faith in all of Scripture. Often referred to as the "Hall of Faith," this chapter highlights men and women of God who overcame obstacles, endured trials, and accomplished great things because of their unwavering trust in the Lord. Their stories demonstrate that faith is not just an abstract concept but a living, active force that enables God's people to prevail in every generation.

With faith in God, you can overcome adversity. With faith, you can succeed despite the odds. Faith makes you a conqueror and gives you victory when defeat seems certain. Faith lifts you to the place where you become the head and not the tail. Jesus confirmed this truth in Matthew 19:26, declaring that with God, all things are possible.

What Faith Is

Hebrews 11:1 defines faith as "the substance of things hoped for, the evidence of things not seen." Faith is a confident trust that God will do what He has promised, even when we cannot see how He will do it. Faith is believing and trusting God to fix your situation, even when you have no proof of how He will bring it to pass.

Faith is also universal in its principle. Every person on earth lives by faith in some form. While not all believe in the true and living God, people place faith in deities, objects, systems, or even themselves. What sets believers apart is the object of our faith. Our faith is anchored in God, who is eternal, powerful, and faithful to His promises. The fact remains that in spite of your mistakes, faults, and shortcomings, you can overcome the odds when you put your faith in Him.

Faith in In-Spite of is Needed to Worship God

Hebrews 11:4 points to Abel as an example of faith in worship. Abel offered God his best, while his brother Cain withheld and gave less than his best. God accepted Abel's sacrifice but rejected Cain's because worship without wholehearted devotion is unacceptable.

To believe in God is to offer Him your best worship. Worship is more than words. It is a sacrifice. It is giving God your best time, your best praise, your best offering, and your best devotion. Matthew 16:26

reminds us that withholding from God for the sake of personal gain profits nothing, for it can cost us our very souls.

Faith motivates and energizes people to worship God even when life is difficult. In spite of trials, in spite of challenges, faith drives us to lift our voices, raise our hands, and give our hearts in worship to the Lord. The questions we must ask ourselves are: What worship sacrifice am I making unto God? Am I giving Him my best or my leftovers? True faith will always offer God the best.

Faith in In-spite of is a Must to Walk with God

Faith is also essential for walking with God. Hebrews 11:5 records that Enoch pleased God and was taken up without experiencing death because his faith led him to walk closely with the Lord (see also Genesis 5:24). Walking with God requires more than mere belief. It demands daily trust and fellowship with Him.

Paul affirms this truth in 2 Corinthians 5:7, teaching that Christians are faith walkers, not sight walkers. Walking by faith means trusting God even when the path is unclear, even when circumstances are difficult, and even when opposition arises.

We must each examine our testimony. Are we walking with God or simply going our own way? Are we using our time to please Him or to please ourselves? Jesus warned in Matthew 7:21-23 that not everyone who claims to know Him will enter His kingdom, but only those who do the will of the Father. The lesson is clear: faith that pleases God is a faith that walks daily with Him. Do not be in the dismissed crowd—be among those whose walk of faith pleases the Lord.

Faith in In-spite of is Needed to Work for God

Faith is also required for working for God. Hebrews 11:7 highlights Noah, who obeyed God's command to build the ark. His generation had fallen into sin and corruption (Genesis 6:5–6), yet Noah trusted God and worked faithfully. By faith, he built the ark for the saving of his household, even though he had never seen rain like what God promised. His work was evidence of his faith.

James 2:14–17 reminds us that faith without works is dead. If we claim to believe but never act on that belief, our faith is empty and useless. Noah's example demonstrates that true faith inspires action. Faith in God is not passive; it moves us to obey, to serve, and to build according to His Word, even when the world around us doubts.

Final Word: Faith That Worships, Walks, and Works

Faith in spite of difficulties, in spite of doubts, and in spite of obstacles is the kind of faith that pleases God. It is a faith that worships God with the best of our hearts and lives. It is a faith that walks daily in step with Him, trusting His guidance. And it is a faith that works, moving us to action and obedience.

Hebrews 11:1–7 reminds us that faith is the key to living a victorious life. In every circumstance, faith anchors us in God's promises and propels us forward into His purposes. Hold on to faith despite everything, for it is the substance of your hope and the evidence of the God you cannot see but who is always at work on your behalf.

Lesson 21
What You Say

Scripture: Proverbs 15:1

The Power of Words in Relationships

Ineffective communication is one of the greatest challenges in human relationships. Saying the wrong thing at the wrong time, or saying nothing when words are needed, can lead to misunderstanding, broken trust, and even destroyed relationships. This truth applies to every area of life: marriage and family, work environments, church fellowship, and friendships.

Communication is not limited to words alone. Your tone of voice, gestures, facial expressions, nonverbal habits, and the timing of your response all play a role in shaping how your message is received. Every word you speak has the potential to either strengthen or weaken the relationships God has placed in your life. Proverbs 15:1 reminds us that "a soft answer turneth away wrath, but grievous words stir up anger." What you say, and how you say it, matters deeply in every relationship.

Lesson One: What You Say Can Extinguish or Escalate Anger

Solomon, the preacher of wisdom, makes it clear in Proverbs 15:1 that words can either calm anger or inflame it. Every time you are angry or someone is angry with you, you are faced with a choice. You can speak with kindness and godliness, or you can respond with harshness, profanity, or hurtful statements. The choice you make will determine whether the situation is resolved peacefully or escalates into conflict.

Paul reinforces this principle in Ephesians 4:29, encouraging believers to speak words that build others up rather than tearing them down. In Colossians 3:8, he instructs us to put away anger and filthy language. God does not hold us accountable for the words or actions of others, but He does hold us accountable for what comes out of our own mouths. The language you choose and the behavior you display are your responsibility.

Your response shapes the outcome of any conversation, and that outcome will influence the health of the relationship. A gentle response extinguishes anger, while harsh words add fuel to the fire.

Lesson Two: What You Say Can Wound or Heal

Words carry great power. They can act like a two-edged sword, with the ability to heal or to wound. Your words can build up or tear down, encourage or discourage, start a fire or put one out, bring sadness or spark joy, create tears or inspire laughter.

James 1:26 reminds us that those who claim to be religious but fail to control their tongues deceive themselves, and their religion is worthless. In other words, careless speech undermines the very faith we claim to live by. Proverbs 12:17-18 also teaches that truthful words bring healing, while rash words can pierce like a sword.

God gave us the ability to communicate, not so we could harm others, but so we could bring comfort and encouragement to those who are hurting. Your words are tools. Use them to heal, to strengthen, and to give hope.

Lesson Three: What You Say Can Destroy Life or Give Life

Proverbs 18:21 declares that life and death are in the power of the tongue. Just as a carpenter's tools can be used to build up or to tear down, the tongue can be used as a weapon of destruction or as an instrument of healing. The words you speak can either breathe life into someone's spirit or crush them under the weight of negativity.

The impact of your words is profound. A single harsh statement can scar a relationship for years, while a single encouraging word can lift someone out of despair. This is why it is so important to guard your speech. Friendly advice: never be guilty of assassinating someone's character with profanity or abusive language. If you cannot say something good, it is better to say nothing at all.

Lesson Four: What You Say Can Inspire or Deceive

Words also have the power to inspire truth or to spread deceit. They can create peace or provoke conflict, relieve stress or increase it. Proverbs 24:28 warns against deceiving others with our lips. Honesty must guide our speech, for deception undermines trust and destroys relationships.

To ensure your words inspire rather than deceive, practice wise counsel. Speak in ways that help others rather than harm them. Fill your mind with wisdom so that your speech reflects thoughtfulness and clarity. Learn to listen before speaking, and think carefully about your words. Avoid speaking too much, for excessive words often lead to regret. Speech that is intentional and truthful becomes a source of inspiration for others.

Final Word: Guarding the Tongue

The tongue can be one of the most dangerous parts of the body. It has the power to heal or to harm, to bless or to curse. That is why God gave it two natural fences: your teeth and your lips. Sometimes the wisest thing you can do is to keep your tongue behind those fences.

Proverbs 15:1 teaches us that soft words can turn away wrath, while harsh words stir up anger. Every believer must learn to speak in ways that honor God and build others up. What you say is not just about communication. It is about testimony. Your words reflect your heart, and your heart reflects your walk with God.

Lesson 22
Tips for Authentic Relationships

Scripture: John 13:34

Building Relationships That Last

The Bible is filled with principles that guide us in building and maintaining authentic relationships. These principles are not only for the sake of spiritual growth but also for enhancing our everyday connections with family, friends, spouses, significant others, and even those we consider enemies. Authentic relationships require effort, humility, love, and intentionality. By applying biblical wisdom, we can develop relationships that reflect God's heart and bring strength rather than strife.

Tip One: Love Like Jesus Loves

In John 13:34, Jesus commanded His followers to love one another just as He has loved us. This standard of love goes far beyond human affection. It is sacrificial, unconditional love. Jesus knew that loving others would be difficult, which is why He gave us His own example.

To love like Jesus means accepting people as they are without trying to force them into our own mold. Romans 5:8 reminds us that God demonstrated His love for us by sending Christ to die for us while we were still sinners. Loving others in this way means seeing them through God's eyes and treating them with dignity and respect. Authentic love is not based on perfection or performance but on the decision to love despite flaws.

Tip Two: Seek to Understand Each Other

Solomon, the wise preacher, taught that in all our pursuits we should seek understanding (Proverbs 4:7). Relationships falter when people refuse to understand one another. Understanding requires more than simply spending time together. It demands active listening and empathy.

The great Yogi Berra humorously captured this truth when he said, "You can hear an awful lot by just listening." James 1:19 reinforces this principle by encouraging believers to be quick to listen, slow to speak, and slow to anger. True understanding is making what matters to another person important to you because that person is important to you. When you value understanding, you create space for deeper connection, trust, and harmony in your relationships.

Tip Three: Hold True to Your Commitment

Commitment is a cornerstone of authentic relationships. It implies loyalty, fidelity, and a willingness to work through challenges rather than walking away when things get difficult. Real commitment means standing by each other in both the best and worst of times.

Ruth provides a powerful example of loyalty in Ruth 1:16-17, where she declares her unwavering commitment to Naomi. In the New Testament, Paul instructs husbands and wives to submit to one another in love and to mirror the relationship between Christ and the church (Ephesians 5:21-33). These examples remind us that commitment builds trust and demonstrates genuine care.

Friendly advice: Be as committed to your spouse, significant other, or friend as you would desire them to be committed to you. Commitment must be mutual for relationships to thrive.

Tip Four: Show Respect

Aretha Franklin made it plain in her timeless song when she spelled out what every relationship requires: R-E-S-P-E-C-T. Respect is foundational to love, trust, and commitment. Without respect, even the most promising relationship will crumble.

Respect is not about elevating yourself or assuming you are the most important person in the relationship. Paul addresses this in Romans 12:3, warning against arrogance, and in Philippians 2:3, where he calls believers to value others above themselves. Respect means honoring others, listening to their perspective, and treating them with kindness and dignity.

Relationships without respect often devolve into abuse, whether physical, emotional, or spiritual. Lack of respect for God can also disrupt family life and personal relationships. When respect is absent, love cannot flourish.

Tip Five: Practice Forgiveness

Forgiveness is vital for authentic relationships. It means releasing resentment, anger, and the desire for revenge, choosing instead to extend grace. Jesus modeled this powerfully on the cross when He prayed, "Father, forgive them, for they do not know what they are doing" (Luke 23:34). His example teaches us that forgiveness is not about excusing wrong but about freeing ourselves from the burden of bitterness.

Matthew 6:14–15 warns that refusing to forgive others hinders our own forgiveness from God. Holding on to grudges keeps us stuck in the past and prevents healing. Authentic relationships cannot survive without forgiveness. It is the oil that keeps love from drying out and relationships from breaking down.

Forgiveness is more for your benefit than for the person you forgive. As long as you cling to resentment, you carry a heavy burden. Letting go allows you to put down that weight and move forward in freedom.

Final Word: The Path to Authentic Connection

Authentic relationships require love, understanding, commitment, respect, and forgiveness. Without these biblical principles, relationships become shallow, broken, or strained. With them, however, relationships thrive and reflect God's love in a way that blesses others and honors Him.

The tongue, the heart, and the actions of each believer must work together to cultivate relationships that glorify God. By following these principles, we can build connections that are not only meaningful but also enduring.

Lesson 23
The Shield of Faith

Scripture: Ephesians 6:16

The Purpose of Ephesians

Paul wrote the epistle to the Ephesians to encourage and strengthen the saints in the church at Ephesus. His letter had several purposes. First, he wanted to remind them to walk together in the spirit of oneness and unity. Second, he emphasized that Christ is the center of the universe and that the church will always remain united in Him. Third, Paul revealed God's eternal purpose for the universe, showing how that purpose is being worked out through the church.

Scholars and theologians have often referred to Ephesians as the "Queen of the Epistles." It carries the weight of a masterful sermon, holding readers spellbound with its truth. It also reads like a heartfelt prayer, drawing believers into the presence of God. Finally, it closes like a doxology, lifting the soul into worship and leaving the reader with a deeper sense of God's majesty.

When we come to chapter 6, Paul shifts his focus to the reality of spiritual warfare. The Holy Spirit makes it clear through Paul's words that living the Christian life in this fallen world is a battle. The battle is not against flesh and blood but against spiritual forces of evil (Ephesians 6:12). Because of this, Paul instructs believers to put on the whole armor of God (Ephesians 6:11, 13). Among the pieces of armor, he highlights the shield of faith, found in verse 16, as a vital part of spiritual protection. The question then arises: why must believers put on the shield of faith?

Faith Is Essential to Please God

The first reason we need the shield of faith is that it is impossible to please God without it. Hebrews 11:6 makes this truth undeniable: "Without faith it is impossible to please Him." Faith is not optional in the life of a believer. It is the foundation of our relationship with God.

The example of Enoch demonstrates this clearly. Hebrews 11:5 records that Enoch pleased God, and the reason he did so was because of his faith. His life was a testimony that walking with God requires complete trust. Without faith, no amount of good deeds, intellect, or personal effort will satisfy God. Faith is what connects us to Him and allows us to live in a way that pleases Him.

Faith Protects Against the Fiery Darts of the Enemy

The second reason believers need the shield of faith is for protection against the attacks of Satan. Paul describes these attacks as fiery darts, meant to wound, discourage, and destroy. Satan is not a myth but a real enemy of God's people. First Peter 5:8 warns that he prowls around like a roaring lion, seeking whom he may devour. Jesus Himself described the enemy as a thief whose mission is to steal, kill, and destroy (John 10:10).

The shield of faith becomes our defense against these attacks. Just as a soldier in ancient times used a shield to block arrows and fiery missiles, believers use faith to extinguish the lies, temptations, and accusations of the enemy. When Satan whispers fear, faith reminds us of God's promises. When he throws darts of doubt, faith reminds us of God's power. When he stirs discouragement, faith lifts our eyes to the God who can deliver. Faith is the believer's covering in the heat of battle.

Faith Guards Against Doubt

The third reason for the shield of faith is to protect us from doubt. Doubt, left unchecked, can erode trust in God and weaken our spiritual walk. To doubt Jesus is to question His existence or His ability to act. Thomas, one of the disciples, doubted the resurrection until he saw the risen Lord for himself. His doubt eventually turned to faith, but his story reminds us how destructive doubt can be (John 20:24–29).

Doubt undermines our confidence and often leads to anxiety, low self-esteem, and even depression. Spiritually, doubt hinders growth, weakens faith, and can open the door to unbelief. It is important to distinguish between the two. Doubt is the questioning of faith, the uncertainty of the believer. Unbelief is the absence of faith, the condition of those who reject God altogether.

The shield of faith protects us from slipping into doubt and unbelief. It reminds us to trust God even when we do not see the outcome, to believe His promises when circumstances look impossible, and to hold firm when the enemy seeks to shake our confidence.

Final Word: A Faith That Cannot Be Shaken

Faith is not only a shield but a song in the believer's heart. It strengthens us to stand, protects us from the enemy, and keeps us from the grip of doubt. Faith testifies with boldness: "You can't make me doubt Him, for I know too much about Him." When faith burns within us, we can proclaim with confidence, "I've got the love of Jesus in my heart. I feel the fire burning in my soul. Jesus, Jesus, Jesus!"

The shield of faith is not just a piece of armor; it is the believer's lifeline in the battle of life. With it, we please God, withstand the enemy, and rise above doubt. Hold it high, trust in the Lord, and let your faith declare victory in every circumstance.

Lesson 24
The Whole Armor of God

Scripture: Ephesians 6:11-17

The Reality of Spiritual Warfare

As Christians, we must never forget that we have a dangerous adversary. Satan, the devil, is constantly working to weaken our faith and drag us into destruction. His goal is clear: to steal, to kill, and to destroy (John 10:10). Each day, believers are engaged in a spiritual battle, not against flesh and blood, but against demonic forces determined to oppose God's people.

In Ephesians 6:11–17, Paul instructs the church to prepare for this battle by putting on the whole armor of God. He makes it clear that we cannot fight in our own strength. Instead, we must be strong in the Lord and equipped with the spiritual weapons God provides. The enemy is a schemer (2 Corinthians 2:11), a stalker (1 Peter 5:8), a deceiver (Revelation 12:9). He ensnares (2 Timothy 2:26), hinders (1 Thessalonians 2:18), harasses (2 Corinthians 12:7), and attacks with fiery darts of temptation (Ephesians 6:16). Because of this, believers must stay alert, remembering that the weapons of our warfare are not physical but spiritual (2 Corinthians 10:3–4).

Paul outlines the armor of God as the believer's defense against the enemy's attacks. Each piece has a purpose, and together they prepare us to stand firm in faith.

The Belt of Truth

Paul begins in Ephesians 6:14 with the belt of truth. Truth is the foundation of the Christian faith. To put on the belt of truth is to commit to honesty, integrity, and living by the Word of God. Jesus declared in John 8:32 that the truth makes us free, while Satan, in John 8:44, is described as the father of lies.

Wearing the belt of truth means resisting Satan's deception and refusing to live by falsehood. It secures every other part of the armor, keeping the believer grounded in what is real and eternal. Without truth, every other piece of armor is unstable.

The Breastplate of Righteousness

Paul also speaks of the breastplate of righteousness (Ephesians 6:14). This breastplate protects the heart and vital organs of the believer, symbolizing the righteousness given to us through faith in Christ. When we live in obedience to God, we safeguard our hearts against the corruption of sin.

This righteousness is not earned by our works but given by God through Christ. As Paul explains elsewhere, it transforms us into new creations, positioning us to live in holiness (Ephesians 4:23–24). Putting on the breastplate means guarding our hearts and minds, choosing to live rightly before God, and walking in His commands with joy and purpose.

The Shoes of the Gospel of Peace

In verse 15, Paul describes the shoes of the gospel of peace. Just as soldiers needed sturdy footwear to march forward with stability, believers must stand firm in the readiness that comes from the gospel. These shoes symbolize not only the peace we receive from God but also our readiness to share that peace with others.

The gospel brings stability to our steps. It keeps us from stumbling in confusion and gives us direction in the midst of chaos. Hebrews 13:20-21 affirms that the God of peace equips believers to do His will. With the shoes of peace, we are prepared to spread the message of Christ and to stand firmly in our convictions when challenges come.

The Shield of Faith

Paul then points to the shield of faith (Ephesians 6:16). Faith is our defense against the fiery darts of the enemy. Satan aims darts of doubt, fear, temptation, and discouragement, but faith extinguishes them. A soldier's shield was not passive; it was raised actively in battle to block incoming attacks.

In the same way, faith is active trust in God's promises. Proverbs 3:5 instructs us to trust the Lord with all our hearts. Faith is not simply a belief in God's existence but a daily reliance on His power, wisdom, and faithfulness. With faith, we can stand firm against Satan's schemes.

The Helmet of Salvation

The helmet of salvation, found in verse 17, protects the believer's mind. Our greatest battles often occur in our thoughts, where Satan seeks to plant doubt and confusion. The helmet of salvation secures our confidence in Christ, reminding us of our eternal hope and the assurance of God's promises.

When we wear the helmet, we live with the mindset of victory, not defeat. It changes the way we see trials because we know our future is secure in Christ. Ephesians 4:24 describes this as putting on the new man, which is created in righteousness and holiness. To wear the helmet of salvation is to live daily with an eternal perspective.

The Sword of the Spirit

Finally, Paul describes the sword of the Spirit, which is the Word of God (Ephesians 6:17). Unlike the other pieces of armor, the sword is offensive. It allows believers to take the fight to the enemy, cutting down lies and temptations with the truth of Scripture.

Hebrews 4:12 describes the Word of God as living and active, sharper than any double-edged sword, able to penetrate even the deepest thoughts and intentions of the heart. The Bible is not just a book to read. It is a weapon to wield. When Jesus was tempted in the wilderness, He responded to Satan's attacks with the Word of God. We, too, must learn to use Scripture as our defense and offense in spiritual warfare.

Final Word: Standing in Victory

The armor of God is not only symbolic. It is the believer's lifeline in the midst of battle. Each piece equips us to stand against Satan's schemes and to walk in victory. Truth secures us. Righteousness guards us. Peace guides us. Faith shields us. Salvation assures us. And the Word empowers us.

Your Bible is not just a devotional tool; it is an active weapon of warfare. Use it daily, courageously, and faithfully. With the whole armor of God, you can stand firm, resist the enemy, and walk in the victory already won for you through Jesus Christ.

Lesson 25
Different Kinds of Conflict

Scripture: Leviticus 19:18

"Thou shalt not avenge, nor bear any grudge against the children of thy people, but thou shalt love thy neighbour as thyself: I am the LORD" (v.18).

Introduction

From the beginning of time, conflict has been part of the human story. The Bible records conflicts between individuals, families, and even nations. Both the Old and New Testaments speak to the reality of conflict and how God's people are to respond. Leviticus 19:18 reminds us that while conflict is inevitable, revenge and grudges have no place in the life of a believer. Instead, we are commanded to love our neighbor as ourselves. To better understand this truth, we must recognize the different kinds of conflict we encounter in life and how Scripture teaches us to handle them.

Internal Conflict

Internal conflict is the struggle that takes place within a person's own heart and mind. It is often invisible to others, but it can weigh heavily on the soul. A clear biblical example is Jacob's wrestling with God in Genesis 32:24–32. Before meeting his brother Esau, Jacob struggled physically and spiritually, wrestling through his fears and his need for forgiveness. Similarly, Peter experienced internal conflict when he denied Jesus three times (Matthew 26:69–75). His heart longed to be loyal, but his fear of association with Jesus led him into denial.

Internal conflict can arise in several ways. Sometimes it happens when a person cannot decide which task or responsibility should take priority. Other times, it comes when personal convictions and values clash with obligations to family, work, or even faith. Such conflicts often produce stress, guilt, or dissatisfaction, leaving a person feeling stuck and unable to move forward. When left unresolved, internal struggles can block spiritual growth and hinder emotional well-being.

Interpersonal Conflict

Interpersonal conflict occurs when disagreements, rivalries, or misunderstandings take place between individuals or groups. Genesis 13 provides a powerful example when conflict arose between the herdsmen of Abraham and Lot. Instead of allowing the strife to destroy their relationship, Abraham took three deliberate steps to resolve it. He took the initiative to address the problem, he offered Lot the first choice of land, and he prioritized family peace over personal gain (Genesis 13:7–12).

Interpersonal conflict can arise for many reasons. Differences in personality, cultural backgrounds, or core values can lead to friction. Miscommunication, pent-up frustrations, or unresolved anger can also fuel conflict until it eventually "comes out sideways" in unhealthy ways. While interpersonal conflict is often painful, it also provides an opportunity for growth when approached with humility, forgiveness, and a commitment to peace. Abraham's example shows us that taking initiative and placing relationships above personal advantage can bring lasting resolution.

Spiritual Conflict

Spiritual conflict is the battle believers face against temptation, sin, and the forces of evil. Unlike internal or interpersonal struggles, spiritual conflict directly challenges our faith and requires reliance on God's strength. Matthew 4:1–11 records Jesus' temptation in the wilderness, where He faced three powerful tests. First, Satan tempted Him to turn stones into bread (v.3–4). Second, he urged Jesus to throw Himself from the temple to test God's protection (v.5–7). Third, he offered Jesus worldly power in exchange for worship (v.8–10).

Jesus overcame each temptation by relying on the Word of God. This shows us that spiritual conflict cannot be won by human strength or reasoning but by standing firmly on Scripture and trusting in God's promises. For believers, spiritual battles are unavoidable, but victory comes when we lean on the truth of God's Word and depend fully on His power.

Final Word: God's Purpose in Conflict

Conflict is not without meaning. While it often causes discomfort, it can serve a greater purpose. Conflict allows us to glorify God, to serve others, and to grow to be more like Christ (1 Corinthians 10:31; 11:1). Internal struggles push us toward God's guidance. Interpersonal conflicts challenge us to practice humility and forgiveness. Spiritual battles strengthen our dependence on God's Word and power.

Conflict, when approached with faith, is not merely a problem to endure but an opportunity to reflect Christ in our words, actions, and relationships.

Lesson 26
Five Biblical Steps to Resolving Conflicts

Scripture: Matthew 18:15-17

The Importance of Peacemaking

Conflict is a reality in every area of life. It arises in homes, workplaces, schools, governments, communities, and even within the church. Left unresolved, conflict can grow into bitterness, hatred, and division. This is why learning how to resolve conflict is one of the most vital ministry skills any believer can have. Unresolved conflicts not only damage relationships. They damage the testimony of the church and hinder the work of God's kingdom.

First John 4:20 makes it clear that we cannot claim to be in harmony with God if we are out of harmony with one another. Conflict resolution, therefore, is not optional for believers. It is a spiritual responsibility. Jesus outlined a process in Matthew 18:15-17 for addressing conflicts, and these principles guide us toward peace, reconciliation, and spiritual maturity.

Step One: Take the Initiative

The first step in resolving conflict is to take the initiative. Do not wait for the other person to come to you, and do not pretend the conflict does not exist. Jesus calls us to be peacemakers (Matthew 5:9). Taking initiative often requires courage, especially when fear or pride tells us to remain silent.

Loving our enemies is not a suggestion but a command (Matthew 5:44). Love drives out fear (1 John 4:18), giving us the courage to make the first move toward peace. When your love for God and others outweighs your fear of rejection or discomfort, you will take the step to restore relationships.

Step Two: Confess Your Part of the Conflict

The second step is to acknowledge your part in the conflict humbly. Pride will trap you in a cycle of blame and unforgiveness if you wait for the other person to act first. Even if the other person bears 99 percent of the blame, you are still responsible for confessing your own one percent.

Jesus taught in Matthew 7:3–4 that before pointing out the speck in someone else's eye, we must first remove the plank from our own. Often, broken relationships are like traffic jams, stuck in a standstill. Sometimes, one simple sentence like "I'm sorry" is enough to clear the way forward. Humility opens the door to reconciliation.

Step Three: Listen for the Hurt

The third step is to listen for the hurt behind the words or actions. Hurt people often hurt others. When someone lashes out at you, it may not be about you at all. It may come from wounds inflicted by others in their past. This is why listening is so important.

James 1:19 teaches us to be quick to listen, slow to speak, and slow to anger. God gave us two ears and one mouth for a reason: we should listen twice as much as we speak. By listening to understand rather than listening to respond, we can often uncover the root of the hurt and begin to heal the relationship.

Step Four: Tell the Truth in Love

The fourth step is to tell the truth, but to do so in love. Ephesians 4:15 reminds us to "speak the truth in love." Truth without love comes across as harsh and is often resisted. Truth wrapped in love is more easily received. The goal is not to win an argument but to restore a relationship.

Revelation 21:8 warns us that liars will not inherit eternal life. Therefore, honesty is non-negotiable for followers of Christ. At the same time, truth must be spoken with compassion. Jesus Himself said in John 8:32, "And ye shall know the truth, and the truth shall make you free." The truth, shared with love, brings freedom and healing.

Step Five: Focus on Reconciliation, Not Resolution

The final step is to focus on reconciliation rather than resolution. There is a difference between the two. Reconciliation restores the relationship, while resolution means eliminating all disagreements. In reality, two people may never fully agree on every issue. But they can choose to love one another, respect one another, and walk in unity despite differences.

Jesus blesses those who are peacemakers (Matthew 5:9). Peacemakers do not avoid conflict, nor do they escalate it into war. They seek to rebuild trust and re-establish connection. You can disagree without being disagreeable. You can value the relationship above the argument.

Final Word: Choosing the Path That Honors Christ

Conflict will always be present in our world. The question is not whether conflict will come, but how we will respond to it. We can ignore it, which would make it worse. We can escalate it, adding fuel to the fire. Or we can let the Lord use us as instruments of peace.

Resolving conflict God's way brings glory to Him, strengthens relationships, and makes us more like Christ. When we take initiative, confess our part, listen with compassion, speak truth in love, and prioritize reconciliation, we reflect the heart of the Savior who came to reconcile the world to Himself. That is the decision that truly honors Jesus.

Lesson 27
Sin

Scripture: Genesis 2:15-17; Genesis 3; Romans 5:12; James 1:13-15

The Root of the World's Brokenness

What is the worst thing in the world today? Some might say it is mass shootings, drug addiction, corrupt politics, racism, cancer, broken families, economic instability, or nations at war. Yet while these are devastating, they are not the ultimate problem. The worst thing in the world today is sin.

Sin is the root cause of every tragedy, injustice, and broken reality we see in the world. It is because of sin that our world is filled with hatred, violence, and suffering. Genesis 1:26–27 reminds us that humanity was created in the image and likeness of God, designed to reflect His character and glory. God breathed into the first human the breath of life, and man became a living soul (Genesis 2:7). We were created as both material beings, with bodies formed from dust, and immaterial beings, with souls and spirits given by God. As His image bearers, we were meant to mirror His holiness. Yet sin corrupted this design, distorting God's image within us and introducing brokenness into every area of life.

Lesson One: We Sin When We Transgress the Laws of God

The Bible defines sin as lawlessness, a direct disobedience to God's commands (1 John 3:4). Scripture is filled with examples of individuals who failed to do what was right and reaped the consequences of their disobedience.

Cain, the firstborn of humanity, committed the first murder when he killed his brother Abel out of jealousy (Genesis 4:8). King David, though a man after God's heart, sinned greatly when he committed adultery with Bathsheba, the wife of Uriah (2 Samuel 11:3–4). Peter, one of Jesus' closest disciples, denied the Lord three times out of fear (Matthew 26:69–75). Paul, before his conversion, persecuted the church and approved of the stoning of Stephen (Acts 8:3). Ananias and Sapphira lied to the Holy Spirit about the proceeds from the sale of their property and were judged severely (Acts 8:1–10).

These examples remind us that none of us is exempt from sin or its penalty. Hebrews 9:27 makes clear that judgment is inevitable. Every person will one day stand before God and give an account for their life.

Lesson Two: Sin Entered the World Through Man

Genesis 3 records how sin first entered the world. Eve's encounter with the serpent reveals the gradual steps that lead to disobedience. She listened to the devil's voice (Genesis 3:1), lingered too long in the place of temptation (Genesis 3:2), allowed God's Word to be twisted in her hearing (Genesis 3:4–5), fell into Satan's trap by desiring what she saw (Genesis 3:6), and finally yielded to the temptation by eating the forbidden fruit (Genesis 3:6). Afterward, she gave it to Adam, and when he ate, their eyes were opened. Shame, guilt, and fear entered the human story, and they tried to cover their nakedness and hide from God (Genesis 3:6–7).

From that moment, sin became part of the human condition. Romans 3:23 declares that all have sinned and fallen short of God's glory. Romans 3:10 reminds us that none are righteous—not one. Adam's disobedience opened the door for sin to spread to all humanity, as Romans 5:12 explains: "By one man sin entered into the world, and death by sin; and so death passed upon all men."

Lesson Three: Sin Has Consequences

Sin is never without consequences. Romans 6:23 teaches that "the wages of sin are death." Adam and Eve experienced this firsthand. Their sin brought separation from God, eviction from the garden, and the certainty of physical death (Genesis 3:16–24).

Cain's sin of murder led to God's judgment, making him a fugitive and wanderer upon the earth (Genesis 4:12). David confessed that his sin was ever before him, following him everywhere he went (Psalm 51:3). King Saul lost his life because he disobeyed God's command (1 Chronicles 10:13-14). The lesson is clear: sin may seem appealing in the moment, but its consequences are devastating and inescapable.

You may get by with sin for a season, but you will not get away with it. God is holy, and sin always brings separation and judgment.

Final Word: Taking Sin Seriously

Sin is not something to be taken lightly. It is the greatest problem facing humanity. Charles Spurgeon once said, "Too many think lightly of sin and therefore think lightly of the Savior." When we diminish the seriousness of sin, we diminish our need for the cross.

The good news is that while sin brings death, God has provided life through Jesus Christ. The same verse that declares the wages of sin are death also declares that the gift of God is eternal life through Christ Jesus our Lord (Romans 6:23). Only by recognizing the seriousness of sin can we truly appreciate the greatness of salvation.

Pastoral Self-Care

Lesson 28
A Divine Cure for Anxiety

Scripture: Psalms 37:3 thru 7

The Burden of Anxiety

Someone once said that the best way to live a long life is to get someone else to do your worrying for you. Another writer compared worry to a rocking chair: it gives you something to do, but it does not get you anywhere. These descriptions capture the futility of anxiety. It consumes energy, robs us of peace, and offers nothing in return.

Anxiety can be defined in several ways. It is a feeling of uneasiness or nervousness, a mental and physical state of negative expectation, and an uncomfortable worry about what might happen. We live in what many call the Age of Anxiety. Government corruption, rising crime, drugs in our schools and homes, the killing and imprisonment of young men, racism and injustice, financial struggles, and broken healthcare systems all contribute to the heavy burden of worry.

The truth is, people go to bed worrying. They wake up worrying. They spend the day dwelling on problems only God can solve. Anxiety is real, and being a Christian does not exempt us from it. In fact, Satan uses anxiety as a weapon to weaken our trust in God

128

and to rob us of joy. Yet Scripture gives us a cure. In Psalm 37, David offers a five-step prescription for overcoming anxiety and reclaiming peace.

Step One: Trust in the Lord (Psalm 37:3)

The first step is to trust in the Lord with all your heart. Trusting God means believing He will provide a solution to your problems even when you cannot see the way forward. Throughout Scripture, we see examples of such trust. The three Hebrew boys did not worry about being thrown into the fiery furnace because they believed God could deliver them (Daniel 3:16–18). Abraham trusted God to provide a ram in place of his son Isaac (Genesis 22:7–8). David testified that throughout his life, he had never seen the righteous forsaken (Psalm 37:25).

Satan uses anxiety to keep us from trusting God. But when we place our trust in Him, fear loses its grip, and we gain confidence that God is working on our behalf.

Step Two: Delight Yourself in the Lord (Psalm 37:4)

The second step is to delight in the Lord. To delight in Him is to find joy and contentment in His presence, regardless of circumstances. Paul expressed this attitude in Philippians 4:11, where he said he had learned to be content in every situation. Delight comes from living according to God's Word, which serves as both a lamp to our feet and a light to our path (Psalm 119:105).

There is nothing sweeter for the believer than the Word of God. It teaches us wisdom, brings salvation, and shapes us into holiness. A dusty Bible does not scare the devil, but a believer who delights in and lives by the Word of God is powerful against him.

Step Three: Commit Your Way to the Lord (Psalm 37:5)

The third step is to commit your way to the Lord. To commit means to surrender, which includes giving up your habits, traditions, and ways of doing things over to Him. It means acknowledging His authority and seeking His will in every area of life. Proverbs 16:3 teaches us to commit our works to the Lord and trust Him with the outcome.

Job is an example of this commitment. He lost his wealth, livestock, servants, and even his children. He was struck with painful boils and abandoned by friends who failed to comfort him. His wife even urged him to curse God and die. Yet Job declared, "Though He slay me, yet will I trust Him" (Job 13:15). Commitment does not eliminate adversity, but it anchors us in God's faithfulness. As 1 Peter 5:7–9 reminds us, we are to cast our cares on the Lord and trust Him to handle our case.

Step Four: Rest in the Lord (Psalm 37:7a)

The fourth step is to rest in the Lord. David echoes the invitation of Jesus in Matthew 11:28, where He promises rest for the weary and burdened. Rest means releasing today's and tomorrow's worries into God's hands and sleeping in peace, knowing He is in control.

If God cares for the birds of the air, He will surely care for His children (Matthew 6:26). Resting in the Lord frees us from carrying burdens we were never meant to bear. It reminds us that God is working even when we are asleep.

Step Five: Wait on the Lord (Psalm 37:7b, 34)

The final step is to wait on the Lord. Waiting is often the hardest discipline. When frustration rises and people mistreat us, our natural reaction is to fight back or retaliate. Yet David and Isaiah, both teach us that the one who waits on the Lord will see His deliverance (Psalm 27:14; Isaiah 40:31).

Waiting is not passivity. It is active faith. Instead of wasting energy in anger or revenge, we are called to transfer that energy into trust, patience, and hope. Waiting allows God to work in His time and in His way.

131

Final Word: The Prescription for Peace

Anxiety may be real, but so is God's cure. Trust in Him. Delight in His Word. Commit your ways to Him. Rest in His care. Wait on His timing. These steps form a divine prescription that not only calms anxious hearts but also strengthens faith.

When you follow this pattern, you can face life's uncertainties with confidence, knowing that God is faithful to carry your burdens and bring peace to your soul.

Lesson 29
How to Improve
Your Self-Esteem

The World's Obsession with Image

We live in a culture that places extreme value on outward appearance and external success. Billions of dollars are spent every year on products and procedures that promise youth, beauty, and strength. People chase titles, wealth, and recognition, doing whatever is necessary to gain praise and remain in the spotlight.

But what happens when those things fade or are taken away? What happens when the super-athlete becomes confined to a wheelchair? What happens when the supermodel gains weight or ages beyond society's standard of beauty? What happens when the intelligent lose their cognitive ability after a stroke, or when a superstar ends up in jail or addicted to drugs? What happens when a successful career suddenly comes to an end?

For many, their self-esteem collapses with the loss of these external markers. They fall into frustration, discouragement, and depression. They begin blaming themselves or others for their misfortune, forgetting that true self-worth is not built on temporary things.

Understanding Self-Image and Self-Esteem

We all carry a mental picture of ourselves: how we look, what we are good at, and what our weaknesses might be. This picture forms our self-image, which is simply our personal perception of who we are.

Closely tied to self-image is self-esteem, which refers to how we value, accept, and love ourselves. Healthy self-esteem means recognizing your worth, appreciating your skills, and being secure in your identity without being controlled by the opinions of others. On the other hand, low self-esteem often leads people to feel unloved, dependent on the approval of others, and willing to compromise who they are just to be accepted.

Building healthy self-esteem requires shifting the focus away from external approval and toward God's truth about who you are. From a biblical perspective, Scripture provides clear principles for cultivating self-worth that is secure, lasting, and rooted in God.

Principle One: Know Who and Why You Were Created

The first step in improving self-esteem is knowing your origin and purpose. David acknowledged in Psalm 24:1 2 that the earth and everything in it belongs to the Lord. Isaiah declared that humanity was created for God's glory (Isaiah 43:7). You are not an accident, and your value does not come from society's standards. You were handcrafted by God for His glory.

When you recognize that your life has a divine purpose and that you were created to reflect God's image, your sense of worth naturally increases. Self-esteem rises not from what you achieve or how you look, but from the truth that you are valuable because you belong to God.

Principle Two: Stop Speaking Negatively About Yourself

The second step is to silence the negative voice that diminishes your worth. Many people struggle with believing they are incapable, unworthy, or inadequate. This mindset often keeps them from fulfilling God's call.

Jeremiah the prophet faced this struggle. When God called him, he responded with doubt, saying he was too young (Jeremiah 1:6–7). Yet God reminded him that before he was conceived, He had already set him apart for a purpose (Jeremiah 1:5). The lesson is clear: self-doubt does not define you—God's call does.

Improving your self-esteem requires speaking truth over your life. Philippians 4:13 reminds us that we can do all things through Christ, who strengthens us. Replacing negative words with words of faith and confidence in God's promises will build self-esteem and strengthen your identity in Christ.

Principle Three: Stop Living in the Past and Move Forward

The third step is to stop allowing past failures or mistakes to dictate your present and future. Paul is a clear example of this. Before his conversion, he was an enemy of Christ and a persecutor of the church (Acts 8:1–3; 9:1–2). Yet when he encountered Christ, he refused to remain chained to his past. Instead, he pressed forward, declaring, "Forgetting those things which are behind, and reaching forth unto those things which are before, I press toward the mark" (Philippians 3:13–14).

Paul understood that his past did not define him; God's grace did. Likewise, when you choose to let go of yesterday's mistakes and live in the freedom Christ provides, your self-esteem will rise. Your past becomes a testimony, not a prison.

Final Word: A Biblical Foundation for True Self-Worth

Improving self-esteem is not about chasing beauty, success, or approval. It is about recognizing your God-given identity, speaking truth over your life, and refusing to let the past control your future. When you know you were created by God for His glory, when you stop speaking negatively, and when you press forward in faith, you will discover a self-esteem that is strong, resilient, and unshakable.

Lesson 30
Notes on Pastoral Self-Care

Scripture: Mark 12:30-31

Why Self-Care Matters for Pastors

Pastoral self-care is essential for both the well-being of the pastor and the health of the ministry. It involves caring for one's physical, emotional, mental, and spiritual needs to ensure balance and sustainability. Too many pastors push themselves to exhaustion, believing that tending to their own needs is selfish. In reality, self-care allows pastors to serve God and others more effectively.

Jesus made this clear in Mark 12:30–31, teaching that we are to love God with all our heart, soul, mind, and strength, and to love our neighbor as ourselves. Notice that loving others well requires loving ourselves in a healthy, godly way. Pastors cannot pour into others if they are spiritually, physically, and emotionally depleted.

Pastoral Priorities and Balance

Many pastors know in their minds that God should come first, followed by family, and then ministry. However, in practice, these priorities are often neglected. The demands of preaching, counseling, and

137

leading can easily consume every moment, leaving little energy for one's family or personal walk with God.

It must be remembered that God did not call pastors to sacrifice their health or their families on the altar of ministry. A pastor who ignores self-care eventually risks burnout, resentment, and strained relationships. Worse still, neglecting self-care may harm the very church they are trying to serve, as an unhealthy leader cannot lead effectively.

Principle One: Reserving Family Time

Pastors must intentionally set aside quality time with their families. Ministry will always be demanding, but boundaries must be drawn. Family time should be placed on the calendar and treated as non-negotiable. Emergencies may arise, but not every call or request from the church qualifies as an emergency.

When pastors consistently neglect their families, they risk damaging marriages, alienating children, and creating resentment. Family time should not be viewed as optional. It is part of the pastor's calling. As the saying goes, if you do not take care of your home, someone else might step in to fill that void. Protecting family time is essential to building trust, love, and stability at home.

Principle Two: Protecting Privacy

Pastors often live under the constant gaze of others, but they, too, need private space. Protecting privacy helps maintain a sense of normalcy for both the pastor and their family. This may mean avoiding a church office within the home, maintaining separate phone lines, and setting boundaries for when church members can reach out.

Family events such as dinners, game nights, or special celebrations should not be interrupted by unannounced visits. A weekly day off should be established and respected by the congregation. When pastors protect their privacy, they give their families the message that they are valued and not constantly competing with church responsibilities.

Principle Three: Clarify Expectations

Many congregations have unspoken and sometimes unfair expectations of pastors and their families. For instance, some may expect the pastor's spouse to lead specific ministries or the pastor's children to be perfect role models. If these expectations are not addressed early, they create unnecessary stress and strain.

It is important for pastors to clarify roles and responsibilities. The pastor alone is called to serve in that official capacity; the spouse and children are not automatically assigned roles within the church.

Congregations should not expect more from a pastor's family than they do from any other family in the church. Clear communication can prevent resentment and division.

Principle Four: Building Friendships

Pastors often avoid close friendships out of fear of betrayal or because of the dual relationship between leader and congregant. However, isolation is dangerous. Every pastor needs trusted friends who can provide support, encouragement, and accountability.

Research shows that many pastors lack even one close friend to share their burdens with. While caution is necessary, trusted relationships are vital for emotional health. Pastors should seek out safe, reliable friendships either within or outside the church that provide a source of strength in both good and difficult seasons.

Principle Five: Seek Help When Needed

Perhaps one of the greatest struggles pastors face is seeking help for themselves. Those who spend their lives ministering to others often feel uncomfortable admitting their own struggles. Yet pastors are not superhuman. They too face stress, exhaustion, and emotional burdens.

When you feel drained, overwhelmed, or unable to think clearly, it is not a sign of weakness to seek help. Professional counseling, spiritual guidance, or medical support may be necessary. Seeking help is not a failure. It is a wise step toward health and longevity in ministry. Ignoring warning signs only leads to deeper burnout and greater damage.

Final Word: Ministry Should Strengthen, Not Suffocate

The work of ministry is demanding, but it should not suffocate the pastor's soul. Instead, it should be a place of strength and joy. Pastors must remember that loving God, loving their families, and loving themselves in healthy ways are not in conflict with ministry. They are the foundation of it.

Without proper self-care, ministry can become destructive rather than life-giving. But with balance, boundaries, and intentional care, pastors can lead effectively while protecting their health and their families. Ministry should strengthen the soul, not destroy it.

Self-Care Scriptures to Read

Exodus 34:21 – Rest is commanded as part of God's design.

Proverbs 17:22 – A joyful heart brings healing.

Matthew 6:34 – Do not be anxious about tomorrow.

Matthew 11:28 – Jesus promises rest for the weary.

Romans 12:2 – Renewal of the mind is essential.

Ephesians 5:29 – Care for your own body is God-honoring.

Philippians 4:6-7 – Prayer brings peace in place of anxiety.

Colossians 3:2 – Keep your focus on things above.

1 Peter 5:7 – Cast all your cares on Him.

3 John 1:2 – God desires us to prosper and be in health.

Lesson 31
Discipleship in the
21st Century

Scripture: St. Matthew 5:19

The Call to True Discipleship

Discipleship is the process of being transformed into a committed learner and follower of Jesus Christ. It is not merely about attending church but about allowing God to take ownership of your life (Luke 9:23). True discipleship is about surrender: submitting your body, mind, and spirit to God so that He can shape you into the image of Christ. Without surrender, there can be no true transformation, and without discipleship, the mission of the church will fall short.

Why Discipleship Matters

Discipleship is critical because, without it, both leadership and membership fail to fulfill their role of winning and maturing souls for Christ. The church was not designed to be a social club or an event-driven institution. It was created to advance the Kingdom of God. This advancement happens through teaching (Matthew 28:19–20), preaching (Mark 16:15–16), witnessing (Acts 1:8), praying (Luke 18:1), loving (John

13:34–35; 15:12), fellowship (Acts 2:42), and giving (Malachi 3:8–10; 2 Corinthians 9:6–8).

The early church grew in both numbers and spiritual maturity because it embraced Jesus' model of discipleship (Acts 2:41–47). To be a disciple is to live daily according to His Word (John 8:31; 13:15).

What We Should Know About Ministry

Many misunderstand ministry as simply attending worship, giving tithes, serving on boards, or participating in auxiliaries. While these things are important, they do not capture the full meaning of ministry. True ministry is about demonstrating God's mercy, serving Christ with humility, and fulfilling the assignment He has given you. It means being willing to get your hands dirty to help others become clean. Ministry is saying "yes" to God's invitation to join Him in advancing His kingdom. However, the ministry cannot function without resources—both financial and human.

What We Should Know About Evangelism

Evangelism is at the heart of discipleship. It is proclaiming the gospel to the ends of the earth, even when it comes at great cost (Matthew 28:19–20; Acts 1:8). Evangelism is serving as Christ's ambassador, representing the Kingdom of God in a world of darkness. It is both personal and practical: families sharing Christ with their families, believers feeding the hungry, caring for the sick, and humbly serving others. Evangelism is love in action, communicating both the message and the nature of Christ. Like ministry, evangelism requires resources to be effective. Without investment, outreach cannot reach its full potential.

What We Should Know About Discipleship

Discipleship is not a program or a one-time event; it is a lifelong commitment to follow Jesus. It involves nurturing and maturing others through teaching, equipping believers with godly principles, and training them to serve alongside Christ. Discipleship is about transformation, that is, helping people move from simply hearing about Jesus to actively obeying His commands.

Effective discipleship is integrated, not segregated. It includes senior adults, youth, teenagers, and young adults, uniting all generations in the family of God. At its core, discipleship uses the Word of God to mature and equip believers so that they not only remain in the church but also participate in the work of ministry. Like evangelism and ministry, discipleship requires the right investment of resources—time, people, and finances.

The church must be willing to invest financial resources to get the human and physical resources to evangelize, train disciples, and do the work of the ministry.

145

In Short:

No money = No evangelizing (winning souls for Christ)

No money = No disciple-making (equipping and maturing believers to follow Christ)

No money = No personnel and physical resources to do ministry

The Challenge of the 21st Century Church

Too often, the modern church has abandoned Jesus' model of discipleship. In many congregations, especially within the African American church context, the focus has shifted to Sunday morning worship, annual programs, and fundraising efforts. Beautiful buildings are constructed, but many lack classrooms or facilities to support discipleship and spiritual growth. As a result, churches become event-driven rather than disciple-making communities.

Jesus came not only to die for our sins but also to show us how to make disciples. His model was relational, intentional, and transformational. Discipleship requires more than listening to sermons or attending lectures. It demands teaching, modeling, encouragement, conversation, and accountability. All grounded in a living relationship with Jesus and other believers. Without these relationships, discipleship cannot thrive.

Discipleship as a Transforming Experience

Discipleship transforms every part of life. To be a disciple requires:

- A Transformed Mind: Believing what Jesus believed (Romans 12:1–2; Philippians 2:5).
- A Transformed Character: Living the way Jesus lived (Matthew 4:2–4).
- A Transformed Relationship: Loving as Jesus loved (John 13:34–35).
- A Transformed Habit: Training as Jesus trained (Matthew 16:24).
- A Transformed Service: Ministering as Jesus ministered (Mark 10:45).
- A Transformed Influence: Leading the way Jesus led (Philippians 2:3).

Discipleship is not just about knowledge; it is about becoming more like Christ in every dimension of life.

Practical Suggestions for Making Disciples

To make disciples effectively, churches must create environments that support learning, growth, and transformation. Some practical steps include:

- Developing discipleship training for all age groups.
- Easing rigid dress codes to create a welcoming environment.
- Loving and accepting people as they are.
- Celebrating the achievements and milestones of members.
- Eliminating favoritism in the church.
- Investing in the necessary financial, human, and physical resources.
- Planning activities that engage all age groups.
- Updating technology for communication and ministry.
- Involving every age group in meaningful participation.
- Ending a culture of criticism and replacing it with encouragement.
- Using the church facility for more than worship and Bible study, making it a hub for community and discipleship.
- Transforming worship from a routine experience into one that is dynamic, empowering, and life-changing.

Final Word: Returning to Jesus' Model

The effectiveness of the church in the 21st century depends on its commitment to true discipleship. Without it, the church risks becoming shallow, event-focused, and ineffective in retaining souls. But when the church embraces Jesus' model, it produces mature believers who love, serve, and lead like Christ.

Discipleship is not optional. It is the heartbeat of the church's mission. It is the difference between temporary followers and lifelong laborers for the Kingdom of God.

Lesson 32
Evangelism

Scripture: John 3:16

The Foundation of Evangelism

For clarity, evangelism is not about forcing people into faith through guilt or fear. It is not beating people over the head with the Gospel or engaging in endless debates about who is going to Heaven and who is going to Hell. Evangelism is not fiery preaching designed to scare people into submission, nor is it the quoting of scripture simply to show one's knowledge.

The foundation of evangelism is love. As Jeremiah 31:3 reminds us, God has loved us with an everlasting love. John 3:16 makes it clear that God's love for the world moved Him to give His only begotten Son. John 15:13 declares that there is no greater love than one who lays down his life for his friends. Romans 5:8 reveals that while we were still sinners, Christ died for us. Galatians 2:20 echoes this truth by affirming that Christ loved us and gave Himself for us. Evangelism flows out of this divine love—it is motivated by love, rooted in love, and carried out with love.

What Evangelism Is

Evangelism is the act of going forth to share the gospel in the power of the Holy Spirit while trusting God with the results. It is telling others about the life, ministry, and teachings of Jesus Christ, and inviting them to become His followers. Evangelism is not manipulation. It is faithfully presenting the good news and leaving the response in God's hands.

We see this clearly in the story of Philip and the Ethiopian eunuch (Acts 8:26–35). Philip, guided by the Holy Spirit, explained the Scriptures to the eunuch. The eunuch believed and was baptized. Evangelism is simply sharing the message of Jesus in such a way that others are given the opportunity to respond in faith.

Throughout our lives, we have often heard sermons on the Great Commission (Matthew 28:18 20). Jesus charged His disciples to make disciples by teaching and preaching the Gospel. This mandate is not optional, nor is it limited to pastors and preachers. Every believer has been given the responsibility to participate in evangelism.

The Responsibility of Every Believer

Evangelism is not the sole responsibility of ministers, evangelists, or pastors. It is the calling of every Christian. Each follower of Jesus is commissioned to share the good news within their families, communities, workplaces, and beyond.

However, to evangelize effectively, believers must be equipped for the task. Christian education, corporate worship, and collective prayer are the key avenues where believers are trained, encouraged, and empowered to share their faith. The more we are equipped through the Word, the stronger and more confident we become in proclaiming Christ.

Evangelism Helps Keep the Gospel Central

The Apostle Paul, in 1 Corinthians 15:1–3, emphasized the importance of remembering the core gospel message. Evangelism ensures that the church never drifts away from its primary mission. When we evangelize, we are constantly reminded that our purpose is not entertainment, tradition, or self-promotion. It is proclaiming Christ.

Keeping the Gospel central is vital for both the health of the individual believer and the church as a whole. Jesus made it clear in Matthew 7:24–27 that obedience to His Word is the foundation of a life built to last. Evangelism keeps us aligned with this truth, grounding us in the message of salvation and hope.

Evangelism Deepens Our Understanding of Scripture

Solomon, in Proverbs 4:7, urges us to seek understanding. Sharing the Gospel with others forces us to go deeper into Scripture, to study carefully, and to understand what we believe and why we believe it.

This is crucial because Satan distorts and twists the Word of God to lead people astray. Genesis 2:17 records God's clear warning that disobedience would lead to death. Yet Satan contradicted God's truth in Genesis 3:4 by saying, "You shall not surely die." This tactic of twisting Scripture continues today.

Evangelism requires us to know the truth of the Word so we can present it faithfully. As Paul instructed in 2 Timothy 2:15, believers must study diligently to rightly handle the Word of truth. Sharing the Gospel deepens our grasp of God's Word and strengthens our defense against deception.

Evangelism Equips the Saints for Service

Ephesians 4:11–13 teaches that God has placed leaders in the church to equip believers for the work of ministry. Evangelism is not only about reaching the lost but also about equipping the saved. When believers engage in evangelism, they grow in faith, maturity, and commitment.

If we fail to use our God-given gifts and resources to win souls, we are guilty of not being fully committed to Him. Evangelism strengthens the body of Christ by turning passive members into active laborers. It equips saints to serve faithfully, encouraging a cycle of discipleship and multiplication within the church.

Final Word: Love at the Center of Evangelism

At its heart, evangelism is about reflecting the love of God. John 3:16 reminds us that God so loved the world that He gave His only Son. Our ministry to the lost, our willingness to share the Gospel, and our service to those in need all flow from that love. Evangelism is not about arguments or coercion. It is about demonstrating God's love and inviting others into it.

When believers commit themselves to evangelism, they align their lives with the heart of God, and through that love, lives are changed, souls are saved, and the Kingdom of God is advanced.

The Church and Leadership

Lesson 33
Jesus, the Head of the Church

Scripture: Colossians 1:18

Christ as the Head of the Church

To read and study the Bible is to know with certainty that Jesus, God's only begotten Son, is the head of the church. He is the ultimate authority, the foundation, and the source of life for His people. While the church may have human leaders: Bishops, Pastors, and Elders, they are not the supreme authority. They serve as under-shepherds under Christ's leadership. According to both Ephesians 1:22–23 and Colossians 1:18, Jesus is the ultimate authority over all things, including the church. He is the King of kings, and His will is supreme. The church belongs to Him, and its leadership, direction, and mission must reflect His lordship.

Human leaders play a vital role in guiding the congregation, but their authority is valid only when it aligns with Scripture. No pastor, bishop, or elder has authority apart from Christ. They serve to shepherd the flock, but they do so under the authority of the Chief Shepherd.

The Role of the Under-Shepherd

Christian theology teaches that the Bishop, Pastor, or Elder functions as the under-shepherd of the local church. These leaders are entrusted with the care, guidance, and nourishment of the flock, as Jeremiah 3:15 reminds us: "And I will give you pastors according to mine heart, which shall feed you with knowledge and understanding." Yet every under-shepherd must recognize that their authority comes from Christ, and they remain accountable to Him who is the true Head of the Church.

God has not designed His church to operate under competing leadership. Just as it would be unnatural for God to create a two-headed cow, it would be against His plan for the church to be led by multiple competing heads. For this reason, the Pastor is called to lead, while deacons, trustees, officers, and other ministry leaders serve faithfully under the pastor's leadership. This structure preserves unity and reflects the order God established for His people.

Lesson I: Church Leaders and Members Must Understand

Every leader and member of the church must come to a clear understanding of who Jesus is and what His headship means.

- Jesus is the Founder of the Church (Matthew 16:18).
- He is the Head of the Church (Colossians 1:18).
- He has all power, authority, and control over the church (Matthew 28:18–20).
- Believers are subject to Him in everything, both individually and collectively as His body (Ephesians 5:22–24).
- Believers must obey Him (Hebrews 5:9).
- Believers must live their lives according to His teaching (2 John 1:9).

When the church understands this, it keeps Christ at the center of all things, ensuring that both leaders and members serve in humility and obedience to His will.

Lesson II: The Head of the Church Is the Son of God

The church must never forget that its foundation is Jesus Christ, the Son of God. Local church leaders and members are charged with proclaiming to the world that the church does not exist because of human efforts or denominational structures. It exists because of Christ.

When Peter declared in Matthew 16:16, "Thou art the Christ, the Son of the living God," he was making a confession that stands as the cornerstone of the Christian faith. Jesus is not only the founder of the church but also its eternal Lord and Savior.

- Jesus, the Founder of the Church, is the Son of God (John 3:16; 20:31).
- Jesus, the Founder of the Church, is Lord of the Church (Philippians 2:10–11).
- Jesus, the Founder of the Church, is our faithful Intercessor (Romans 8:34).
- Jesus, the Founder of the Church, is our King (Revelation 17:14; 19:16).

Every local congregation must constantly proclaim this truth: the church belongs to Christ, and He alone is its Head.

Lesson III: Jesus the Head of the Church Is Coming Back

The Bible makes it clear, and Christians firmly believe, that Jesus is coming back. John 14:1–3 assures us of this promise, as does 1 Thessalonians 4:16–17 and Revelation 1:7. His return is not a question of "if," but a question of "when." Because of this, it is the responsibility of every believer to live with readiness and anticipation.

Amos 4:12 exhorts us to prepare to meet our God, and Matthew 24:44 reminds us, "Therefore be ye also ready: for in such an hour as ye think not the Son of man cometh." This means living a life that reflects faithfulness, obedience, and alignment with God's will. The return of Christ calls for believers to live with urgency, ensuring that their lives are marked by holiness, service, and readiness.

Final Word

The phrase "Be ye also ready" is more than a command. It is a call to live in a constant state of spiritual preparedness. Jesus is the Head of the Church, and as His followers, we are called to live in submission to His authority, proclaim His lordship, and anticipate His return. The church is not ours to control or shape according to human desires. It is Christ's church, founded on His sacrifice, governed by His Word, and sustained by His Spirit.

To live as members of His church is to recognize His authority, follow His example, and prepare ourselves daily for His coming.

Lesson 34
Worship: A Lifestyle and Not an Event

Scripture: Romans 12:1-2

The True Meaning of Worship

What would your church building become if the church itself ceased to exist? Would the community even notice its absence? Would the building turn into a storage shed or just another abandoned structure decaying on the roadside? These questions force us to reflect on the true purpose of the church and the importance of authentic worship.

To keep the church alive and vibrant, the focus must always be on mission and ministry. Jesus understood His mission clearly, and He carried it out through active ministry (Luke 4:18–19; Mark 10:45). He also commanded the church to evangelize and make disciples through both internal and external ministries (Matthew 28:19–20). Internally, this means the church must move beyond becoming a place of mere entertainment, ritualistic programs, fundraising, or empty traditions. Instead, the church must return to being the house of prayer, praise, worship, and ministry.

Jesus Himself demonstrated His standard for true worship when He entered the Temple and drove out those who used it for personal profit (Matthew 21:13). This action reminds us that worship is more than an event on Sunday mornings. Worship is about honoring and praising God for who He is and for what He has done and continues to do in our lives (Psalm 95:6–7; Psalm 150:1).

The question we must all ask is this: How do we move from seeing worship as an event to embracing worship as a lifestyle?

Lesson I: Becoming a Living Sacrifice (v.1)

The first step in transforming worship into a lifestyle is to become a living sacrifice. Romans 12:1 urges believers to present their bodies as a living sacrifice, holy and acceptable to God. This requires giving all of ourselves, our time, our talents, our desires, and our daily actions to God's service.

William Barclay once wrote, "Real worship is the offering of everyday life to God." This truth reminds us that worship is not limited to church gatherings or specific moments of singing and prayer. Instead, it is about living every moment for the glory of God. As 1 Corinthians 10:31 teaches, "Whatever you do, do it all for the glory of God."

To become a living sacrifice means surrendering fully to God. It is not about partial commitment but about total dedication to Him in body, mind, and spirit. This surrender is what turns ordinary living into true worship.

Lesson II: Changing the Way You Think (v.2)

The second step is allowing transformation to take place in the way you think. Romans 12:2 reminds us that we must not conform to the patterns of this world but be transformed by the renewing of our minds. Worship as a lifestyle begins in the mind.

You cannot live a life of worship if your thoughts remain shaped by worldly standards. Instead, your mind must be renewed by the Holy Spirit, enabling you to think and act with the mindset of Christ. Philippians 2:5 tells us, "Let this mind be in you, which was also in Christ Jesus." A renewed mind helps us to see life through God's perspective, to desire what He desires, and to live according to His will.

This transformation of thought empowers us to resist temptation, embrace holiness, and view worship not as a weekly obligation but as a daily, ongoing commitment. True worship begins when our thinking changes to align with God's truth.

Lesson III: Submitting Your Will to God's Will (v.2)

The third step to making worship a lifestyle is learning to submit your will to God's will. This daily surrender requires constant prayer, echoing the words of Matthew 6:10: "Thy will be done in earth, as it is in heaven."

When worship becomes your lifestyle, you stop living according to your own desires and begin living according to God's plan for your life. Submission means acknowledging that God's will is greater than your own ambitions or preferences. It means trusting His direction even when it requires sacrifice or leads you away from comfort.

Living this way changes everything. Your choices, your values, your actions, and even your relationships become a reflection of your obedience to God. Worship, then, is no longer an event you attend but a way of life you embody.

Final Word

When worship is transformed from an event into a lifestyle, the believer experiences a powerful shift. No longer is worship confined to a building or a schedule; instead, it becomes a daily act of living in submission, gratitude, and obedience to God. And with this lifestyle of worship comes the promise of everlasting life (1 John 2:17).

Worship that pleases God is not about ritual. It is about becoming a living sacrifice, renewing the mind, and submitting to His will. When these things happen, worship moves from being a performance to becoming a way of life: one that honors God in every moment.

Lesson 35
Serving Together in the Kingdom of God (The Church) Part I

Scripture: I Corinthians 3:9

Why Are There So Many Problems in the Local Church?

One of the major reasons why many local churches experience problems is the mindset of their leaders and members. Too often, people view themselves as bosses rather than servants. This misunderstanding of purpose creates division and hinders the work of the ministry. The truth is that within the Body of Christ, we are all called to serve, not to be served. Jesus made this clear in Mark 10:45 when He declared that He came to minister, not to be ministered unto. Solomon, the wise preacher, reminded us of the importance of seeking both wisdom and understanding (Proverbs 4:5-9). Without this understanding, churches fall into disorder and dysfunction.

Another problem is disobedience, which is sin and a serious threat to the life of any ministry. When church leadership and membership refuse to listen and take heed to what God says, the result is destruction. Disobedience leads to pride, division, and the collapse of spiritual effectiveness.

A third problem is the growing infestation of disrespect within the church. Too often, deacons and trustees rebel against the leadership of the pastor, while pastors themselves sometimes push their own personal agendas. Both behaviors are out of order and sinful (I Corinthians 14:40; Romans 6:23). Instead of working together, these conflicts create strife that damages the testimony of the church in the community.

Ironically, church leaders and members often have no problem submitting to their supervisors at work, yet struggle to submit to the leadership of their pastor within the church (Hebrews 13:17). This inconsistency reveals a deeper issue of spiritual immaturity and misplaced priorities. Every person who accepts Jesus as Savior and unites with a local church must always remember that we are servants and laborers together with God (I Corinthians 3:9).

Responsibilities of Serving Together in the Kingdom of God

Responsibility 1: Serve

Serving is more important than being served. True servant leadership is about dedicating oneself faithfully to the service of God, the church, and the community until death (Luke 22:27-30; Revelation 2:10). A servant leader does not seek position, control, or recognition, but lives to meet the needs of others in the spirit of Christ.

Responsibility 2: Learn

It is not enough to simply have a willingness to serve. Every church member must also cultivate a desire to learn how to serve effectively. Serving without knowledge can lead to confusion and inefficiency. Samuel made this clear when he committed to teaching the people the good and right way (1 Samuel 12:23). Jesus Himself urged His followers to learn from Him (Matthew 11:29). Paul encouraged believers to study diligently to be approved by God (2 Timothy 2:15). Learning equips us to serve with excellence and wisdom.

Responsibility 3: Give

The church and its ministries depend on the faithful giving of its members. Tithes and offerings are not optional but are commanded for the support of the church and its work (Malachi 3:8-10). Jesus reminded His followers that gaining the whole world profits nothing if the soul is lost (Matthew 16:26). Paul added that giving must come from the heart, cheerfully and willingly (2 Corinthians 9:6-7). Leaders and members alike are obligated to give faithfully so that the ministry can flourish.

Responsibility 4: Worship and Praise

Regular participation in worship and praise is essential for all leaders and members. Unless hindered by illness, emergencies, or circumstances beyond their control, servant leaders must be faithful in gathering with the church for worship. Leadership requires example, and no leader can expect their members to be consistent in worship if they themselves are absent. The Psalms remind us that worship is not optional: "Come, let us sing for joy to the Lord… let us bow down in worship" (Psalm 95:1-6). "Praise the Lord. Praise the Lord, you his servants; praise the name of the Lord" (Psalm 113:1). "Let everything that has breath praise the Lord" (Psalm 150:6).

Final Word

The ministry of servant leaders within the church is not about power, prestige, or personal agendas. It is about service.

- It is not a ministry of dictatorship; it is a ministry of service.
- It is not a ministry of popularity; it is a ministry of service.
- It is not a ministry of personal gain; it is a ministry of service.
- It is not a ministry of ruling over people; it is a ministry of serving people.

The church of Jesus Christ functions at its best when leaders and members alike embrace their role as servants, laboring together with God for His kingdom.

Lesson 36
Serving Together in the Kingdom of God
(The Church)
Part II

Scripture: I Corinthians 3:9

The Church Exists for God's Glory

It is important to understand that the church was not established for the glory of men but for the glory of God. The focus of every gathering in the House of the Lord must be on Him and not on the beauty of the building, the furniture, or the fixtures. While these things may be impressive, they are not the reason we assemble. Worship is not about architecture or recognition; it is about exalting God. For this reason, no one should ever enter the sanctuary seeking recognition or honor for their title, position, or personal status. The spotlight in worship must always remain on God and not on us.

The Purpose of the Church

The first lesson to remember is that the church is called out and called together to fulfill the purpose of God on the earth, not just within the walls of a local congregation. Jesus commissioned His followers in Mark 16:15 to preach the Gospel to the entire world, not just their own neighborhoods. This global mandate reminds us that the mission of the church extends far beyond our immediate community and reaches into the world at large.

The second lesson to remember is that the local church functions as a spiritual hospital for sin-sick souls, not as a weekly museum for display. It is a place of healing, forgiveness, and transformation where sinners can confess their sins and acknowledge Jesus as their Savior (Romans 10:9-10). The church is meant to be alive, active, and restorative, not stagnant or ceremonial.

The third lesson to remember is that the head of the church is not the deacons, trustees, or even the pastor. The true head of the church is Jesus Christ Himself (Ephesians 5:23; Colossians 1:18). The Scriptures make clear that the two scriptural offices within the church are the pastor and the deacon. The pastor serves as the overseer, providing spiritual leadership and guidance, while the deacon is chosen to assist the pastor in serving as a servant leader (Acts 20:28; Acts 6:2-3). This order ensures that the church functions under Christ's authority and according to His design.

When Does Ministry Take Place?

Warren W. Wiersbe offers a helpful definition when he says, "Ministry takes place when divine resources meet human needs through loving channels to the glory of God." This definition reminds us that ministry is not about personal recognition or selfish ambition. Instead, it is about allowing the love of Christ to flow through us as vessels of service. If our motivation is anything less than Christ's love—His love for us and our love for Him—then our ministry will fail to truly meet human needs or glorify God. Ministry is not simply about activity; it is about service fueled by love.

The Marks of a Servant Leader

A true servant leader embodies several essential qualities that reflect Christ.

- A servant leader is someone whose mind has been transformed by Christ (Romans 12:1-2). Transformation begins within, shaping how we think, act, and serve.
- A servant leader is someone who remembers the needy (Galatians 2:9-10). Genuine leadership does not neglect the poor, the marginalized, or the hurting. Instead, it prioritizes them, reflecting the compassion of Christ.

- A servant leader is someone who is not seeking a name for themselves but is instead seeking opportunities to serve (Philippians 2:6-8). Just as Jesus humbled Himself, servant leaders live to lift others rather than elevate their own reputation.
- A servant leader is someone who respects and obeys leadership (Hebrews 13:17). Respect for authority and willingness to submit to guidance reflect maturity and unity within the body of Christ.
- A servant leader is someone who denies self and follows Christ daily (Luke 9:23). True leadership begins with self-denial and daily obedience to Jesus, placing His will above personal desires.

Final Word

The church was never meant to be a place for personal power struggles or self-promotion. It was established by God for His glory, to heal the broken, proclaim the Gospel, and raise up servant leaders. When pastors, deacons, and members embrace their role as servants under the headship of Christ, the church thrives. Ministry then becomes the meeting place between divine resources and human needs, accomplished through love and humility.

Lesson 37
A Christ-Centered Church

Scripture: John 15:12

The Purpose of the Church

What will it take for the church to become the kind of church Christ desires? What must we do to truly be a Christ-centered church—loving, caring, and committed—where everyone is welcome? Jesus established the church to be a transformative agent, empowered to evangelize the world through preaching, teaching, and ministry of the Gospel (Matthew 28:19-20; Mark 16:15-16; Acts 1:8; Acts 2:41-47). It was never His intent for the church to function as a private social club, a business center, or a financial institution.

Instead, Christ designed the church to be a hospital for sin-sick souls, which includes every one of us. The church should be a place where both sinners and saints are invited, welcomed, and encouraged to hear a Word from the Lord. It should be the place where believers gather to worship and praise Him together (Matthew 21:12-16; Luke 14:16-23; Psalm 95:6; Psalm 150:6).

Loving and Caring (John 13:34-35; Mark 6:32-44)

The first mark of a Christ-centered church is love. Jesus' ministry was rooted in compassion. It was a ministry that included all people and excluded no one. He declared that the world would recognize His disciples by their love for one another: "By this everyone will know that you are my disciples, if you love one another" (John 13:35).

When Jesus walked the earth, people followed Him not simply because of His miracles, but because of His caring spirit. The story of the feeding of the five thousand illustrates His compassion (Matthew 14:13-21). A Christ-centered church reflects this same love, offering an atmosphere where people feel accepted and cared for.

People will travel great distances, passing dozens of churches, simply because they know they will find a loving, friendly, and caring congregation. On the other hand, they may not be able to explain why, but they immediately recognize when they are not truly loved or welcomed in a church. Love must be the heartbeat of every Christ-centered congregation.

Ministry Focus (Luke 4:18; Matthew 20:20-28)

The second mark of a Christ-centered church is a ministry-focused mission. Jesus was anointed and given authority to minister so that the poor could hear the gospel, the brokenhearted could be healed, the captives could be set free, the blind could receive sight, and the oppressed could be liberated (Luke 4:18). His ministry was not about self-promotion but about serving the needs of others.

To be ministry-focused means treating others as we ourselves wish to be treated (Luke 6:31-35). Matthew 20:20-28 teaches that a Christ-centered ministry is not about titles, positions, or authority. Instead, it is about humble leaders and members serving God faithfully by serving others. True greatness in the Kingdom of God is measured not by how many people serve you, but by how faithfully you serve others.

Prayerful (Luke 18:1)

The third mark of a Christ-centered church is prayer. Jesus directed His followers to always pray and never give up (Luke 18:1). Prayer is the lifeline of the believer and the church. It aligns us with God's will and opens the door for His power to work through us.

The saints of old were correct when they declared, "Prayer is the key to the Kingdom and faith unlocks the door." A prayerless church cannot be a Christ-centered church. Prayer must undergird every decision, every ministry, and every effort of the church. It is through prayer that the church seeks God's direction, intercedes for others, and is renewed in strength.

Final Word

A Christ-centered church is marked by love, ministry, and prayer. Its doors swing wide open on the hinges of welcome, inviting all people regardless of background, status, or past. Such a church is not defined by its programs, its finances, or its facilities, but by its heart for God and its compassion for people.

To be Christ-centered is to love like Jesus, to serve like Jesus, and to pray like Jesus. That is the kind of church the world needs, and that is the kind of church Christ has called us to be.

Lesson 38
Servant Leadership
within the Church

Scripture: St. Mark 10:35-45

What Is Leadership?

Leadership, whether biblical or otherwise, is the ability to influence others. True leadership is not simply about holding a title or position but about shaping the lives of those you lead through your actions and your example. Within the church, leadership takes on an even deeper meaning. It is not about power or recognition but about service.

A servant-leader in the church is someone who humbles himself or herself to serve under the leadership of Christ and others. It means empowering people, meeting needs, and leading by example rather than by force. The question every leader must ask is this: Am I leading in a way that reflects Christ? Am I assisting with church ministries and equipping others to serve and lead like Jesus?

What Can We Learn About Servant Leadership from the Early Church?

Lesson 1: Servant Leaders Follow Christ

(Deuteronomy 13:4; Mark 8:34; Ephesians 5:1-2)

A true servant-leader is first a follower of Christ. Following Jesus means striving to reflect His character, obeying His Word, and making Him the Lord over every decision and action. Paul reminds us in 1 Corinthians 10:31 that everything we do should be done to the glory of God. A servant-leader cannot influence others for Christ if he or she is not first surrendered to Christ. To lead others, you must first be led by Him.

Lesson 2: Servant Leaders, Like Jesus, Meet Needs

(Proverbs 19:17; Matthew 14:15-21; Matthew 25:41-46)

Jesus did not just preach the Word; He also met the physical and emotional needs of people. When the crowd grew hungry, He fed them with bread and fish. In the same way, servant-leaders are called to see the needs around them and respond with compassion. Proverbs 19:17 teaches that when we give to the poor, we are lending to the Lord, and Matthew 25 reminds us that meeting the needs of the least of these is the same as ministering to Christ Himself. Servant leadership is not about position; it is about compassion in action.

Lesson 3: Servant Leaders Address Problems

(Acts 6:1-4)

In the early church, a conflict arose when some widows were being neglected in the daily distribution of food. The Apostles recognized the issue and immediately called the church together to address it. They acknowledged that their primary responsibility was the ministry of the Word, but they also knew that the needs of the congregation could not be ignored. Their solution was to appoint servant-leaders, men full of faith and wisdom, to assist in meeting the needs of the people. This moment highlights the importance of servant leadership as a ministry of problem-solving and practical support. Servant-leaders help ensure that no one is overlooked and that the church functions in unity and love.

Four Facts to Remember About Servant Leadership

Fact 1: To lead requires trust. As Paul wrote in 2 Thessalonians 3:4, leaders must prove themselves trustworthy. Can you, as a church leader, be trusted to carry out the responsibilities you have been given with integrity and faithfulness?

Fact 2: Leadership functions under authority. According to Acts 20:28, church leaders serve under the guidance of the overseer, the pastor, who has been entrusted by God to shepherd the flock. Hebrews 13:17 further emphasizes that leaders are accountable both to their pastor and to the congregation. Servant-leaders are not free agents; they operate under God's order and structure.

Fact 3: Servant leadership is not about titles. When James and John asked Jesus for positions of authority in His Kingdom (Mark 10:35-45), Jesus corrected them by teaching that greatness in the Kingdom of God is not about status or recognition but about serving others. True leadership is measured not by how many people serve you but by how many people you serve.

Fact 4: The pastor cannot do everything. No single leader can carry the entire weight of the ministry. The church needs servant-leaders who are willing to assist in ministry, administration, and outreach. The strength of the church is found when leaders and members serve together, each fulfilling their role in the body of Christ.

Final Word

Servant leadership within the church is not about control, titles, or recognition. It is about following Christ, meeting needs, solving problems, and faithfully serving under God's order. When leaders embrace humility and a servant's heart, the church is strengthened, ministries flourish, and God is glorified.

Lesson 39
Five Inspiring Leadership Lessons from Biblical Characters

Selective Scriptures

The depth of character within the people of the Bible is astonishing. These men and women were not perfect, but through faith and perseverance, they faced challenges that tested their convictions and left behind examples for us to follow. Today's church leaders and laity can learn valuable lessons from these ordinary people who accomplished extraordinary things through their commitment to God. In this lesson, we highlight five of them.

Daniel: Leaders Maintain Determination despite the Consequences

In Daniel 6, we read of a man whose faithfulness to God could not be shaken. Daniel was a respected government official, yet his colleagues grew jealous and sought to destroy him. They persuaded King Darius to pass a law forbidding prayer to anyone except the king himself (Dan. 6:4-9). Daniel knew the risk, but he refused to compromise. He continued his routine of praying to God three times a day (Dan. 6:10). He chose to remain faithful even though it meant being cast into the lion's den.

From Daniel, we learn that spiritual leaders must remain steadfast in their convictions, even when threatened by ungodly and jealous people. Leadership rooted in faith requires determination that does not waver in the face of pressure or danger.

John the Baptist: Leaders Are Not Afraid to Call Out Perpetrators

John the Baptist was known for his boldness. In Matthew chapter 3, as he was baptized in the Jordan and preached repentance, a group of self-righteous religious leaders approached. John did not flatter them nor stay silent. He confronted them directly, calling them a brood of vipers (Mt. 3:7). His commitment to truth was greater than his concern for reputation.

This teaches us that leaders must sometimes speak hard truths and confront hypocrisy, even when it is uncomfortable or unpopular. Genuine leadership is not about pleasing people but about remaining faithful to the message of God.

Jesus: Leaders Are Servants

Perhaps the greatest example of leadership is found in John 13, when Jesus, the Son of God, humbled Himself to wash the feet of His disciples (Jn. 13:4-5). Afterward, He reminded them that if He, their Teacher and Lord, could stoop to serve, then they also were called to wash one another's feet (Jn. 13:12-15). This powerful image of humility and service defined His ministry and demonstrated what leadership in the Kingdom of God truly means.

Jesus showed that leadership is not about titles or authority but about serving others. True leaders use their influence to lift others up, to meet needs, and to follow the example of Christ in humility.

Peter: Leaders Recover from Failure

Peter, one of Jesus' closest disciples, is remembered both for his zeal and for his weakness. In Mark 14, he boldly declared that he would never deny Jesus (Mk. 14:27-31). Yet, in fear, he denied Him three times, just as Jesus had foretold (Mk. 14:66-72). This failure was devastating, but Peter's story did not end there. In John 21:15-17, Jesus restored him, reaffirming his calling and commissioning him to feed His sheep.

From Peter's example, we learn that leaders are not defined by their failures but by how they respond to them. True leaders repent, rise again, and continue to fulfill their God-given assignments. Failure can be a turning point that strengthens character and deepens commitment.

Paul: Leaders Are Enthusiastic About What They Believe

Paul was known for his passion. Before his conversion, his zeal was directed against the church, and he went to great lengths to persecute Christians (Acts 8:3). But after encountering Christ on the Damascus road (Acts 9:3-6, 17-20), Paul redirected that same passion into preaching the Gospel. His enthusiasm and determination carried the message of Jesus across the Roman world.

Paul teaches us that leaders must have a fire within them for what they believe. Leadership fueled by passion and conviction has the power to transform lives and communities. Enthusiasm for Christ compels leaders to persevere despite opposition.

Final Word

The examples of Daniel, John the Baptist, Jesus, Peter, and Paul remind us that leadership in the Kingdom of God is not about prestige or titles but about faithfulness, truth, humility, resilience, and passion. Leaders who embody these qualities inspire others and glorify God through their service. Their lives challenge us to live with conviction, to speak with courage, to serve with humility, to recover from failure, and to lead with passion for the Gospel.

Lesson 40
Empowering Church Leaders
for Kingdom Service

Scripture: St. Matthew 5:1-2; I Corinthians 14:40

The ancient Hebrew community and the first-century Christians left the twenty-first-century church with valuable lessons on biblical and spiritual leadership. Through trials, struggles, and divine encounters, they learned how to build and lead people according to God's will. Today, for the church to remain alive and vibrant, leaders must embrace those lessons from Jesus and the spiritual fore-parents who paved the way.

Every person who has leadership potential must understand that he or she will face trials, tribulations, obstacles, and tests. Leadership ability will always be challenged and put on trial, sometimes by the very people one seeks to love and lead. Even Jesus faced this. Immediately after His baptism and the declaration of God's approval, He was tested by Satan in the wilderness (Mt. 4:1-11). Another reality is that spiritual leaders, whether they are pastors or ministry workers, serve under the leadership of the church and must operate in humility, recognizing their accountability to God and to the body of Christ.

Lesson One: Definitions

Leadership, in its simplest form, is the ability to guide and influence others from one point to another. A leader is someone who influences others to follow. Within the church, leadership is the process of guiding others to accomplish the mission of the church by giving purpose, direction, and motivation. Church administration equips the church to fulfill its mission and organizes resources so that ministry can flourish. Ministry itself is the rendering of service. To minister is to perform deeds that are helpful and necessary, meeting needs inside and outside the church fellowship for the sake of Christ.

Lesson Two: Jesus Was a Servant Leader

C. Gene Wilkes, in Jesus on Leadership, explained that servant leaders take up Jesus' towel of servanthood and meet the needs of others (Jn. 13:1-17). Jesus' ministry was successful because He humbled Himself and became a servant (Mk. 10:42-45). For today's church to thrive, its leaders must also embrace humility and servanthood. Titles do not make leaders; rather, leaders give meaning to titles. A leader who is filled with pride and arrogance is not fit for service and should step aside. Servant leadership is rooted in humility, not recognition.

Lesson Three: Servant Leaders Are Spiritual Leaders

Spiritual leaders are both anointed by God and appointed or elected by the pastor and the church. They are empowered by the Holy Spirit with gifts designed to accomplish God's will. J. Oswald Sanders, in his work on spiritual leadership, emphasized that spiritual leaders are sacrificial leaders, modeling the example of Jesus Christ who gave Himself for the world (Jn. 3:16). True spiritual leadership requires daily surrender to God, as Paul reminded us in Romans 12:1-2. Effective leaders sacrifice their time, energy, resources, and talents for the sake of Christ and His church.

Lesson Four: The Original Purpose for Spiritual Leadership

As Jesus' ministry expanded, it became too much for one individual to handle alone. He appointed twelve disciples with diverse backgrounds to assist Him (Mt. 10:1-4; Mk. 3:13-19; Lk. 6:12-16). Later, He appointed seventy others to spread the message and help with the work (Lk. 10:1). After Pentecost, when the church grew rapidly, needs were overlooked, and the Apostles directed the congregation to select seven men to assist in the ministry (Acts 6:1-7). These men became servant leaders whose purpose was to strengthen and expand the work of the Kingdom.

Lesson Five: The Pre-Requisites for Spiritual Servant Leaders

Those who serve as leaders in the church must meet biblical qualifications. They must be born again (Jn. 3:7), meek and humble (Mt. 5:5; I Pet. 5:5-6), and compassionate (Mt. 20:34). They must love God and people (Mt. 22:37-40), be truthful and not double-tongued (I Tim. 3:8), and live as both hearers and doers of the Word (Jas. 1:22). Leaders must be faithful and dependable (Rev. 2:10), properly trained (Mt. 5:1-2; II Tim. 2:15), and obedient to authority (Heb. 13:17; II Cor. 2:9). They must also be prayerful (I Thess. 5:17; Lk. 18:1), sacrificial (Rom. 12:1-2), and tithers who support the work of God financially (Mal. 3:10).

Lovett H. Weems, in Ten Leadership Lessons from Nehemiah, reminds us that leadership begins with vision. Nehemiah cast the vision, the people confirmed it, and together they committed to the task. Great work for the Kingdom requires the gifts and cooperation of all.

Lesson Six: The Spiritual Chief Executive Officer in the Church

Scripture identifies the pastor as the overseer of the local church (Jer. 3:15; Acts 20:28; Eph. 4:11-13). The pastor's role is far more than preaching on Sundays or teaching Bible study. Pastors are responsible for overseeing worship, ordinances, administration, finances, membership, ministries, and every aspect of church life. Every officer within the church serves under the leadership of the pastor and should not act independently of his or her guidance. The pastor is, in effect, the chief executive leader, carrying the weight of responsibility for the congregation.

Lesson Seven: Spiritual Servant Leaders Assist the Pastor with Ministry

Servant leaders play vital roles in the church. Deacons assist the pastor in spiritual matters and in serving the congregation. Trustees manage the legal and physical affairs of the church and help oversee finances. Clerks or secretaries maintain records, membership lists, correspondence, and calendars. Treasurers act as chief financial officers, handling funds responsibly and ensuring obligations are met. Financial secretaries work alongside treasurers to keep accurate giving records. Ministers of music and musicians provide worship leadership under the pastor's direction. Sunday School superintendents oversee Christian education, while presidents of various ministries organize their work and keep leadership informed. Together, these servant leaders provide structure and support for the church's mission.

Lesson Eight: Spiritual Servant Leaders Work Together as a Team

Leaders within the church should not be divided or working against each other. Instead, they must work together as laborers with God (I Cor. 3:9). Teamwork is essential for the church to function effectively. Unity among leaders fosters unity within the congregation, while division among leaders weakens the entire body.

Lesson Nine: Responsibilities of Spiritual Servant Leadership Team Members

Leadership comes with responsibility. Leaders must serve faithfully, remembering that serving is always more important than being served (Lk. 22:27). They must be lifelong learners, growing in wisdom and learning how to minister effectively (I Sam. 12:23). Leaders are called to give their tithes, offerings, time, and energy to support the church (Mt. 16:26). They must also lead by example in worship and praise, attending services regularly and encouraging others to do the same (Psa. 95:1-6; 113:1; 150:6). Finally, leaders must obey the rules of the church and submit to the authority God has placed over them (Heb. 13:17).

Lesson Ten: Spiritual Servant Leaders Are Caring Responders

True leaders not only guide but also care for the needs of those they lead. Noah responded to God's call by building the ark to save his family and preserve humanity (Gen. 6:13-22). Abraham answered God's call to become the father of a nation (Gen. 12:1-3). Peter, restored by Jesus, was called to feed the flock of God (Jn. 21:15-17). Above all, Jesus Himself responded to the needs of people with compassion, ensuring that no one went away hungry (Mt. 14:15-21). Caring leaders respond because they understand that ministry is about people, not position.

Final Word

Empowering church leaders for Kingdom service means developing leaders who are humble, Spirit-filled, sacrificial, and committed to working together. The church is strongest when its leaders understand their responsibilities, submit to the authority of Christ and their pastor, and serve with compassion. When leaders function in unity and humility, the church fulfills its God-given mission to be salt, light, and a witness to the world.

Lesson 41
Church Administration:
The Church

Scripture: Matthew 16:18

In his book The Church, Edmund P. Clowney defines the church as "the people of God, the assembly and body of Christ, and the fellowship of the Holy Spirit." He further states, "The Lord who calls his church to worship and to nurture also sends it through the centuries and across the continents to witness for him." This definition captures the depth and breadth of what the church is and what it has been called to do.

The Universal Church

God Himself established the church for His purpose. The saved are called to live in fellowship as members of God's family, united in spiritual communities. The word "church," or ekklesia, means "the called out" or "called together" company of baptized believers in Christ. The church is therefore not merely a building or institution, but a people who are alive in Christ and who gather in a spiritual atmosphere to fulfill His purpose.

The New Testament often refers to the church in a universal sense, describing the entire body of Christ across the world. Jesus Himself declared in the Gospel of Mark, "Go ye into all the world, and preach the gospel to every creature" (Mk. 16:15). The universal church is a global fellowship of believers whose mission is to carry out this command.

The Local Church

At the same time, Scripture frequently speaks of the church in a local sense. The local church is made up of a community of believers who gather for worship, instruction, fellowship, and service. Paul, writing to the Corinthians, addressed the local assembly in Corinth with these words: "Unto the church of God which is at Corinth, to them that are sanctified in Christ Jesus, called to be saints, with all that in every place call upon the name of Jesus Christ our Lord, both theirs and ours: Grace be unto you, and peace, from God our Father, and from the Lord Jesus Christ" (I Cor. 1:2-3).

Jesus also made clear the foundation of the church when He said to Peter, "Thou art Peter, and upon this rock I will build my church; and the gates of hell shall not prevail against it" (Mt. 16:18). Both the universal and the local church exist because of Christ, who came to redeem humanity from sin.

The church is both human and divine. It is human because it consists of men and women who bear the marks of human frailty. It is divine because it is the Body of Christ, with Jesus as its head. Scripture establishes two primary offices in the local church: the pastor and the deacon. The pastor is the overseer of the flock, while the deacon assists the pastor by serving as a servant leader (Acts 20:28; Acts 6:2-3).

J. Newton Brown, in A Baptist Church Manual, defines the visible church as "a congregation of baptized believers, associated by covenant in the faith and fellowship of the gospel; observing the ordinances of Christ; governed by his laws; and exercising the gifts, rights, and privileges invested in them by his word." He further clarifies that only scriptural officers are bishops, or pastors, and deacons, whose qualifications and duties are outlined in the epistles to Timothy and Titus.

The Purpose of the Church

The Bible leaves no ambiguity regarding the purpose of the church. The local church exists first and foremost for God and for His glory. Charles Bridges wrote, "The Church is the mirror that reflects the whole brilliance of the Divine character. It is the grand scene, in which the perfections of Jehovah are displayed to the universe." This truth reminds us that the church does not exist for our personal agendas but for the glory of God.

The purpose of the church is lived out in three major ways: through worship, edification, and evangelism. Mark Dever summarized this by saying that the proper ends of a local congregation are the worship of God, the edification of believers, and the evangelization of the world. Each of these purposes serves the greater goal of glorifying God.

Worship

The local church exists to glorify God through worship. When believers gather, worship should be conducted in a decent and orderly fashion, to glorify God. Every worship service is an opportunity for God to speak, to pour out His grace, and to transform lives through His Word. True worship is not about performance or routine, but about exalting God in spirit and in truth.

Edification

The local church also exists to glorify God by edifying one another. This goes far beyond casual conversation or social gatherings. Edification is about encouraging one another, showing love, and holding one another accountable in the faith. As Paul taught, the church grows when every member does its part (Eph. 4:15-16). Tim Chester and Steve Timmis explained it beautifully: "It is in the family of God that I am able to care and be cared for; love and be loved;

forgive and be forgiven; rebuke and be rebuked; encourage and be encouraged." In this sense, every believer is both a giver and a receiver of ministry, contributing to the spiritual health of the whole body.

Evangelism

Finally, the local church exists to glorify God by evangelizing the world. A healthy church must be an evangelizing church. While it is true that the church is a gathering of believers, it is also a place where unbelievers are welcome to hear the gospel and witness it lived out. Churches that neglect evangelism lose their zeal, vitality, and eventually their very identity. D.A. Carson put it bluntly: "Evangelize or die." To evangelize is to fulfill the mission of Christ, bringing light into darkness and hope into hopelessness.

Final Word

The local church was founded by God, exists for God, and exists to glorify His name. Our task is not to reshape the church according to our own desires, but to faithfully embrace God's definition and design for it. The church exists to glorify God through worship, through edification, and through evangelism. In this way, the local church is not merely another human institution. It is God's plan for reaching the world, and it remains the hope of the world.

Lesson 42
Church Administration:
Church Constitution

Scripture: I Corinthians 14:40

Should churches have a constitution? The answer is yes. Every local church should establish and maintain a constitution. A written constitution is not simply a legal document; it is a spiritual and practical necessity that helps ensure the church operates according to biblical principles and in good order. Paul reminds us in 1 Corinthians 14:40 that "all things be done decently and in order," and a church constitution provides the structure for that to happen.

Why Churches Need a Constitution

Efficiency and Organization

A constitution promotes efficiency within the church by outlining its governing structure. It defines the roles and responsibilities of pastors, deacons, trustees, and other leaders. It also sets the requirements for membership and outlines the policies and rules of order for the congregation. In this way, the constitution ensures that leadership and membership understand their responsibilities and can work together without confusion.

199

Direction and Clarity

A church must clearly articulate its mission and methods of operation. A constitution provides the parameters and boundaries for leadership decisions and ministry functions. It includes procedures for elections and appointments of officers, the licensing and ordination of ministers and deacons, and the handling of finances and expenditures. With a constitution, the church has a roadmap for decision-making, ensuring consistency and accountability.

Unity and Testimony

A written constitution helps preserve unity and protect the testimony of the church. There are issues of Christian living and practice that the Bible does not address specifically, yet they may cause division if not handled carefully. Bylaws can guide in these gray areas. For example, a church may choose to include in its bylaws a commitment to abstain from alcohol or other practices that might harm the witness of the congregation. While not necessarily doctrinal issues, these agreements strengthen unity and protect the church's testimony before the world.

Protection and Liability

A constitution and bylaws also protect the church from unnecessary liability. Written policies on church discipline, the screening of youth workers, and other sensitive matters safeguard the congregation and its leaders. These policies serve as a protective shield for both the membership and the leadership, providing clarity on expectations and procedures in times of crisis.

The Purpose of the Church Constitution

Many people may not even realize that most churches already have a constitution. These documents often contain bylaws and policies intended for the well-being of the congregation. A well-written constitution protects members from false accusations, from unbiblical disfellowshipping, and from the danger of any single individual or group gaining unchecked control of the church. It ensures that leadership remains accountable and that the congregation has a shared understanding of expectations and responsibilities.

The constitution should address matters of church discipline and moral conduct. For example, members who openly live in unrepentant sin, such as sexual immorality or habitual law-breaking, must be held accountable to the biblical standard. If such issues arise, the constitution provides the procedures for addressing them, which could, in serious cases, result in disfellowshipping. In all matters, the goal is not punishment, but restoration and the protection of the church's witness.

Order in the Church

It must be remembered that the church does not belong to any one man or woman. The church is the body of Jesus Christ, who declared, "Upon this rock I will build my church, and the gates of hell shall not prevail against it" (Mt. 16:18). He is the Chief Cornerstone, and we are living stones being built into His temple.

For this reason, order is essential. Paul wrote, "For God is not a God of confusion but of peace" (I Cor. 14:33). A church without clear guidelines can fall into chaos and division. For example, constitutions and bylaws may include policies such as requiring that pastors not meet privately with women unless another individual is present, or setting boundaries to protect counseling sessions. These policies safeguard both the one receiving counsel and the one giving it.

The constitution must also clearly state the doctrinal foundation of the church, its beliefs, and its biblical convictions. It should spell out the responsibilities of leaders and members alike and describe procedures for decision-making, conflict resolution, and leadership accountability. In this way, no single person can dominate or misuse the church for personal gain, and the congregation remains aligned with God's will.

Sample Outline for Church Constitution

A church constitution and bylaws outline the church's core beliefs, purpose, and operational procedures. The constitution establishes fundamental principles, while bylaws detail specific rules and guidelines for governance, membership, and other activities. A typical outline includes sections on the church's name and purpose, statement of faith, membership, leadership structure, financial management, and conflict resolution.

I. Constitution: Name and Purpose

This section clearly states the church's official name and its religious purpose and mission.

II. Statement of Faith:

It outlines the church's core beliefs and doctrines, ensuring unity in what the congregation affirms.

III. Affiliation:

It specifies if the church is affiliated with a larger denomination or organization.

IV. Bylaws: Membership:

It defines membership requirements, rights, and the process of joining and leaving the church.

V. Governance Structure:

This section defines the leadership roles within the church, including the responsibilities of pastors, deacons, trustees, and other leaders. It also establishes the procedures for the election, appointment, and removal of officers.

VI. Meetings:

It specifies the frequency and procedures for regular and special business meetings.

VII. Decision-Making:

It outlines how decisions are made, including voting procedures and quorums.

VIII. Financial Management and Accountability:

This section explains how the church manages its finances, including budgeting, accounting, and reporting.

IX. Property Management:

It specifies who owns and manages the church's property.

X. Conflict Resolution:

This section establishes procedures for resolving disputes among members or between members and leadership.

XI. Amendments:

It explains the process for amending the constitution or bylaws when changes are needed.

XII. Other Policies:

Additional policies may be included, such as guidelines for personnel, the use of church facilities, or other matters necessary for the health and function of the church.

Final Word

A church constitution is not merely a legal document but a spiritual safeguard. It provides order, protects unity, outlines responsibilities, and ensures accountability. It allows the church to carry out its mission effectively while maintaining a clear testimony before the world. Above all, it honors God's command that "all things be done decently and in order" (I Cor. 14:40).

Lesson 43
Church Covenant

Scripture: Hebrews 13:20-21

A church covenant serves as a formal agreement among church members, outlining their duties and commitments to God, fellow believers, and the church community.

Having been led, as we believe, by the Spirit of God, to receive the Lord Jesus Christ as our Savior, and on the profession of our faith, having been baptized in the name of the Father, and of the Son, and of the Holy Ghost, we do now in the presence of God, angels, and this assembly, most solemnly and joyfully enter into covenant with one another, as one body in Christ.

We engage, therefore, by the aid of the Holy Spirit, to walk together in Christian love; to strive for the advancement of this church, in knowledge, holiness, and comfort; to promote its prosperity and spirituality; to sustain its worship, ordinances, disciple, and doctrines; to contribute cheerfully and regularly to the support of the ministry, the expenses of the church, and the relief of the poor, and the spread of the gospel through all nations.

We also engage to maintain family and secret devotion; to religiously educate our children; to seek the salvation of our kindred and acquaintances; to walk circumspectly in the world; to be just in our dealings, faithful in our engagement, and exemplary in our deportment; to avoid all tattling, backbiting, and excessive anger; to abstain from the sale and use of intoxicating drinks as a beverage, and to be zealous in our efforts to advance The Kingdom of our Savior.

We further engage to watch over one another in brotherly love; to remember each other in prayer, to aid each other in sickness and distress; to cultivate Christian sympathy in feeling and courtesy and speech; to be slow to take offence, but always ready for reconciliation, and mindful of the rules of our Savior to secure it without delay.

We moreover engage that when we remove from this place, we will as soon as possible unite with some other church, where we can carry out the spirit of this covenant and the principles of God's Word.

Biblical Basis for Covenant

I. Salvation and Baptism

The covenant begins with the believer's foundation: salvation and baptism. John 1:11-12 reminds us that those who receive Christ are given the right to become children of God. Baptism, as commanded in Matthew 28:19-20, is the public act of obedience that unites us visibly with the church. Through these steps, believers declare their identity in

Christ and prepare to enter into a covenant with His people.

II. Duties to the Church

The covenant calls members to walk together in Christian love, as Jesus commanded in John 13:34-35. This love is expressed not only in words but in actions that build up the body of Christ. Believers are urged to strive for the advancement of the church, promoting its prosperity and spiritual vitality (Philippians 1:27).

These duties include sustaining worship, ordinances, discipline, and doctrine. Members are called to give cheerfully and regularly to support the ministry, as Paul taught in I Corinthians 16:2 and II Corinthians 8:6-7. The covenant also emphasizes the importance of carrying one's membership when moving to a new community and continuing in church work wherever God places us (Acts 11:19-21; Acts 18:24-28). This ensures that the church remains alive and active in every generation and every place.

III. Duties of Personal Living

The covenant also outlines personal commitments for daily living. Believers are called to maintain family and private devotion (I Thessalonians 5:17-18), keeping their homes centered on prayer and Scripture. They are charged to educate their children in the faith (II Timothy 3:15; Deuteronomy 6:4-7), passing on a godly heritage.

Evangelism is also a personal responsibility. Every believer is to seek the salvation of others, following the call of Acts 1:8, Matthew 4:19, and Proverbs 11:30. Daily conduct should reflect Christ: walking carefully and wisely (Ephesians 5:15), living without complaint and blamelessly (Philippians 2:14-15), and being honorable before unbelievers (I Peter 2:11-12).

The covenant also warns against destructive behaviors. Believers are to avoid gossip, backbiting, excessive anger (Ephesians 4:31; Colossians 3:8), and to abstain from alcohol as a beverage (Ephesians 5:15). Instead, they are to be zealous for good works and dedicated to advancing the Kingdom of Christ (Titus 2:14).

IV. Duties to Fellow Members

The covenant emphasizes mutual responsibility among members of the body of Christ. Believers are to watch over one another in brotherly love (I Peter 1:22), remembering each other in prayer (James 5:16), and aiding each other in times of sickness or distress (Galatians 6:2; James 2:14-17).

Christian sympathy and courtesy are to be cultivated (I Peter 3:8), ensuring that relationships are marked by kindness and respect. Believers are instructed to be slow to take offense and always ready for reconciliation, mindful of Christ's command to forgive (Ephesians 4:30-32). In this way, the covenant strengthens unity and nurtures peace within the church.

Final Word:

When you commit to abide by the church covenant, you are vowing to a personal relationship with God through the Lord Jesus Christ; a personal relationship with the church; a personal relationship with your family and others; and being a Personal witness for Christ.

Lesson 44
Baptist Church Trustees Training Information

Scripture: Matthew 25:14-30

The role of trustees is essential within the local church. It is a multidimensional position that encompasses a wide array of responsibilities critical to the effective functioning of the congregation. Trustees serve as stewards over the legal, financial, and administrative affairs of the church, ensuring that its mission can be fulfilled and its ministries supported. Without faithful trustees, the church's ability to carry out its spiritual mandate would be significantly hindered.

Lesson One: The Definition of a Trustee in a Baptist Church

The role of a trustee in the Baptist tradition is deeply rooted in the principles of trust, responsibility, and accountability. In essence, a trustee is an individual who has been appointed or elected to oversee the management and stewardship of the church's physical and financial assets. This includes property, buildings, land, financial resources, and other material assets that support the life of the congregation. Trustees ensure that these resources are managed responsibly and in accordance with the church's constitution, mission,

211

vision, and values, all under the leadership of the Pastor.

The role, however, is not merely administrative. It carries profound spiritual and ethical significance. Trustees are expected to uphold the highest standards of integrity and ethical conduct, reflecting the core beliefs of the Baptist faith. Their work extends beyond managing resources to preserving the moral and spiritual witness of the church in the community.

A trustee is not a boss or dictator, but a servant leader. Trustees are appointed to serve the congregation and community by exercising wisdom and sound judgment in their decisions. Their role reflects humility, stewardship, and the willingness to use their talents for the glory of God and the benefit of others.

To fulfill this sacred duty, trustees must:

- Understand the church constitution, mission, and vision.
- Uphold ethical standards in every decision.
- Serve with humility, integrity, and accountability.

Trustees are also called to work closely with the Pastor, deacons, and other leaders, providing counsel and support in matters about church property and finances. Their insights, when coupled with spiritual discernment, help guide the church toward responsible management of its resources.

In short, the position of trustee is not simply a title. It is a sacred duty that requires faithfulness, dedication, and a deep commitment to the principles of God's Word.

Lesson Two: Qualifications of Church Trustees

Trustees play a vital role in the everyday functionality of the church. Their duties include overseeing repairs, managing collections, and guiding the investment and protection of church property under the authority of the Pastor and congregation. Because of these responsibilities, trustees must meet specific qualifications that ensure both spiritual maturity and practical competence.

Qualifications include:

- Must be saved and an active member of the church.
- Must be a person of prayer, always seeking God's guidance in decisions.
- Must support the church financially through tithes and offerings.
- Must be a member in good and regular standing.
- Must possess a sound and healthy business mind.
- Must be faithful, prudent, devoted, and have a good reputation.
- Must be bonded/registered within the Circuit Court of the county or city where the church is located.

- Must report to the Pastor and congregation on all updates or repairs to church properties.
- Must never act independently of the Pastor or congregation.
- Along with the treasurer and financial secretary, must oversee all financial matters of the church and help develop financial policies.
- Must manage all properties and legal affairs of the church in accordance with both civil law and the church's constitution.
- Must supervise the cemetery, fellowship hall, and any other temporal (secular) matters of the church as required by law.

Although the specific office of trustee is not mentioned in the Bible, the principles of stewardship are. Matthew 25:14-30 teaches the importance of being faithful stewards, while I Peter 4:10 reminds us to minister to one another as good stewards of God's grace. Trustees, therefore, serve as modern-day stewards within the body of Christ.

Lesson Three: Key Responsibilities of the Church Trustee

Trustees carry several key responsibilities that are interconnected with both the spiritual and practical life of the church.

1. Property Management

Trustees are responsible for the upkeep and oversight of church property, including land, buildings, and other assets. This includes ensuring safety, functionality, and proper maintenance so that the congregation can worship and serve in a secure environment. Decisions regarding renovations, purchases, or sales of property fall within their responsibilities, always guided by the best interests of the church.

2. Financial Stewardship

Trustees are entrusted with overseeing the financial resources of the church. This includes budget planning, financial reporting, and ensuring accountability in every transaction. They are expected to work closely with the Pastor and financial officers to develop policies that safeguard the financial integrity of the church.

3. Legal Compliance

Trustees must ensure the church complies with all legal requirements. This includes filing necessary documents, meeting state and federal regulations for nonprofit organizations, and ensuring that church operations align with legal standards.

4. Risk Management

Trustees must anticipate and mitigate risks that may impact the church. This includes securing insurance coverage, addressing safety concerns, and ensuring protective measures are in place to safeguard the congregation and property.

5. Community Engagement

Trustees often represent the church in the broader community. By fostering partnerships and participating in outreach efforts, they help extend the church's mission beyond its walls.

6. Advisory Role

Trustees also serve as advisors to the Pastor and church leadership. Their counsel provides balance between spiritual vision and practical management, ensuring decisions are well-informed and responsible.

Lesson Four: Legal and Financial Duties

Trustees bear immense responsibility in safeguarding the church's financial and legal standing.

Financial Stewardship

Trustees work with the Pastor and financial officers to create budgets, monitor spending, and ensure accurate reporting. They protect the financial integrity of the church, ensuring that resources are used wisely to support ministries and outreach.

Transparency and Accountability

Trustees must maintain openness in financial matters. This includes honest communication with the congregation, accurate record keeping, and decisions that prioritize the church's mission over personal interests. Transparency builds trust and ensures confidence in leadership.

Lesson Five: Relationship with Church Leadership

Trustees are not independent authorities. Their role is collaborative, supporting the Pastor and leadership team while carrying out their stewardship duties. They serve as partners in advancing the mission of the church, offering their expertise and insight while remaining under pastoral authority.

Lesson Six: Officers Within the Trustee Ministry

The Trustee Ministry is structured with officers such as the Chair, Vice Chair, Secretary, and Treasurer, with additional officers added as needed. Under the Pastor's leadership, trustees must hold regular meetings and report their activities to the congregation. Written and verbal reports should be presented at business meetings to maintain accountability and transparency.

Final Word

The Trustee Ministry is one of the most vital arms of church administration. Trustees are called to serve with humility, diligence, and integrity, ensuring that the church's resources are preserved and used for the glory of God. Their work is both spiritual and practical, and when done faithfully, it strengthens the church's ability to carry out its mission of worship, discipleship, and evangelism.

Lesson 45
The Role of Church Deacons

Scripture: Acts 6:1-6

According to the New Testament Book of Acts, the ministry of the deacon is first and foremost a ministry of service (Acts 6:1-3). The seven men appointed by the Apostles were not called to oversee or rule the church, but rather to assist the Apostles in practical ministry. Their specific task was to serve by meeting the needs of the widows and others who required help.

In Acts 6, the early church was having problems with what I sometimes call their Welfare Program and Helping Hand Ministry. According to Acts 6 the Grecians made a complaint against the Hebrews because their widows were not being treated equally (Acts: 6:1). To resolve the problem the Apostles called the church together and instructed them to choose (recommend) seven men of honest report, full of the Holy Ghost and wisdom; that they (the Apostles) may appoint to be in charge of the Helping Hand Ministry (Acts 6:3).

It is crucial that those who are appointed as deacons understand that their office is not one of power or authority but of servanthood. A deacon is charged to minister with love, humility, and impartiality, reflecting the character of Christ. When a deacon embraces this role as one of service rather than control, he or she

Lesson I: The Authority of the Deacon

Scripturally, the deacon is a servant of the church who functions under the leadership of the pastor. A deacon's role is not one of dominance or authority but of faithful service to the church body. Kevin J. Conner, in The Church in the New Testament, notes that deacons were delegated by the Apostles in the early church (Acts 6:3). They served under the authority of the elders and were entrusted with the responsibility of caring for the widows and distributing alms to the poor. Their work was not self-directed, and it certainly was not an opportunity to manage or misuse church resources for themselves.

In short, deacons are called to be servants of ministry. Their authority does not come from personal ambition or self-appointment but is derived from the church's recognition of their character, calling, and readiness to serve. Deacons are appointed to specific areas of work within the Body of Christ, and their task is to fulfill those duties faithfully for the glory of God.

Lesson II: The Deacon as a Team Member

Deacons are not meant to operate in isolation. They are team members, working alongside the pastor, other church leaders, and the congregation to ensure that the ministry of the church moves forward in unity.

Their responsibilities extend beyond a title and require a lifestyle of service.

First, deacons are called to serve (Luke 22:27). Service is the very heart of their ministry. Just as Jesus declared that He came not to be served but to serve, deacons are responsible for faithfully serving God, the church, and the community. Their commitment must extend to the end of their lives, carrying a spirit of humility and selflessness.

Second, deacons must be willing to learn (1 Samuel 12:23). A willingness to serve without a desire to grow in knowledge and wisdom will lead to ineffective ministry. Deacons who humbly open themselves to teaching and training will become more effective in meeting the needs of the church. Learning equips them to serve wisely and biblically.

Third, deacons are called to give (Matthew 16:26). The church depends on the faithful giving of its members to sustain its ministries. Deacons, as servant leaders, are expected to set an example by tithing and giving offerings generously. Their giving not only supports the work of the church but also demonstrates their commitment to God's kingdom.

Fourth, deacons must be devoted to prayer, worship, and praise (Luke 18:1; Psalm 95:1-6; 113:1; 150:6). They are called to pray continually and to be regular participants in corporate worship. Their presence and active participation in worship services set the tone for the congregation. Deacons cannot expect those they lead to be faithful in worship if they themselves are absent or disengaged. Leadership is by example, and deacons must model what it means to be a worshipper.

Finally, deacons must learn to obey (Hebrews 13:17). They are to govern themselves according to God's Word, the policies of the church, and the leadership of the pastor. Obedience is not a sign of weakness but of humility and trust in God's divine order for the church. Deacons with a servant's heart who look to Jesus as their supreme model of leadership are the ones who will help the pastor and congregation fulfill the will of God.

Lesson III: The Qualifications of a Deacon

The biblical record is clear about the qualifications of deacons, emphasizing that those who serve in this ministry must meet spiritual, character, and domestic standards.

Spiritual Qualifications include being born again (John 3:1-7) and demonstrating obedience to Christ through baptism (Acts 2:38). Deacons must be filled with the Holy Spirit (Acts 2:1-4; 6:3; Ephesians 5:18), and they must hold firmly to the mystery of the faith with a clear conscience (1 Timothy 3:9-13). They are also required to be full of wisdom and faith (Acts 6:3), qualities that enable them to make godly decisions and to minister with discernment.

Character Qualifications call for a life of integrity. Deacons must be reverent, serious-minded, and sincere in spirit (1 Timothy 3:8; Titus 2:2, 7). They must not be double-tongued or given to gossip (1 Timothy 3:8; James 1:8; Psalm 12:2). They must avoid drunkenness (1 Timothy 3:8; Proverbs 20:1) and must not be greedy or driven by a desire for dishonest gain (1 Timothy 3:8). Deacons are to be blameless and above reproach (1 Timothy 3:10), with an honest report and good reputation in both the church and community (Acts 6:3; 16:1-2).

Domestic Qualifications stress the importance of faithfulness in family life. A deacon must be the husband or wife of one spouse, avoiding unfaithfulness or bigamy (1 Timothy 3:12). They must manage their household well, setting an example for their children and family (1 Timothy 3:12-15). The spouse of a deacon must also be grave, not a slanderer, but sober and faithful in all things (1 Timothy 3:11). A deacon's home life is a reflection of their ability to lead and serve in the church.

Lesson IV: Advice for Young and New Deacons

For young and newly appointed deacons, it is essential to remember that the diaconate is not a competitive ministry. It is not meant to create rivalry between the pastor and the deacons or between the deacons and the congregation. There is no biblical foundation for such competition. Instead, deacons are called to serve in harmony with the pastor and church, working together for the glory of God.

To thrive in this ministry, deacons should begin by embracing their identity as servant leaders. Be faithful to what you were appointed to be—a deacon called to serve the church with humility and love. Commit yourself to prayer, lifting your pastor, his family, and the church continually. Recognize your role and "stay in your lane," fulfilling your responsibilities as a deacon without trying to assume the role of the pastor.

Support the church financially with your tithes and offerings, and encourage others to do the same. Lead the congregation in supporting the pastor and his family both spiritually and financially. Stand behind the pastor's recommendations and decisions, understanding that unity strengthens the body of Christ.

Serve with a positive attitude. Do not approach ministry with negativity or anger, and do not use worship services or meetings as a platform to display frustration. Respect the pastor's leadership, and participate in deacon and leadership training at least once or twice a year to continue growing in your role. Avoid cliques and divisions within the church. Stand firmly on biblical principles, even when it means disagreeing respectfully.

In all things, remember that your service is to God first. Spiritual growth is essential to your effectiveness. To grow spiritually means engaging in prayer, study, and consistent discipline, always to draw closer to God and focus less on self. When deacons serve in this way, they see the needs of the church clearly, love those they are called to minister to, and follow Christ daily.

Lesson 46
Empowering Deacons, Trustees, and Associate Ministers for Kingdom Service

Scripture: St. John 13:12-15; I Corinthians 14:40

The ancient Hebrew community and its leaders left the 21st-century church with vital lessons on spiritual leadership. Through personal encounters, struggles, and divine intervention, they learned how to build nations and lead God's people out of bondage into the Promised Land (Gen. 12:1-5; Ex. 3:1-10). They were successful because they sought the will of God and led according to His direction. The same is true for the church today. The leadership of the 21st-century church will only be effective if it follows the biblical model and ministers in alignment with the will of God. This lesson is designed to empower deacons, trustees, and associate ministers for Kingdom service by answering five important questions.

Question One: What Is Biblical Leadership?

Don N. Howell, Jr., in his book Servants of the Servant, defines biblical leadership as taking the initiative to influence people toward growth in holiness while passionately promoting the extension of God's

Kingdom in the world. Biblical leadership is not about power, control, or self-promotion. Rather, it is about shaping others through godly influence, helping them mature in faith, and equipping them to be active participants in advancing the Kingdom. At its core, biblical leadership requires humility, obedience, and a willingness to follow Christ's example of service.

Question Two: Who Are We?

Like Abraham, Moses, and the leaders of ancient Israel, church leaders today are not called to be rulers or dictators. Instead, they are called to be servants of the Servant, Jesus Christ. We step out of order when we demand that the membership serve us or fulfill our personal agendas. Our responsibility is to guide, influence, and encourage God's people to do ministry in accordance with His will. Jesus Himself declared that He came not to be served but to serve, and to fulfill the will of His Father (Mk. 10:45; Jn. 6:38). Leaders who see themselves as servants will uplift and empower others, ensuring that the church remains faithful to its God-given mission.

Question Three: What Is the Ministry of Deacons?

Joseph R. Rogers, in Church Leadership: The Pastor and the Deacon: Servants of God, to the People of God, identifies three reasons why churches need deacons.

First, deacons exist for church growth (Acts 6:1a; 4:4). As the early church expanded through preaching, teaching, praying, and outreach, the Apostles realized they needed help meeting the growing needs of the congregation. They appointed seven men to assist in ministry, allowing the work to continue without being hindered. The same remains true today—deacons are called to assist the pastor in meeting the spiritual and physical needs of the church.

Second, deacons help resolve conflict within the church (Acts 6:1b). When the Grecian widows complained that they were being neglected compared to the Hebrew widows, the Apostles appointed the seven men to handle the matter fairly. Deacons today are called to be peacemakers, helping pastors mediate disputes and ensuring that fairness, justice, and love guide the church.

Third, deacons exist to free up the pastor for prayer and the Word (Acts 6:2-4). The Apostles recognized that they could not be consumed with daily disputes and still fulfill their calling to preach and pray. By delegating responsibilities to deacons, they remained focused on their primary calling. Similarly, deacons today should make sure their pastor is not weighed down with trivial matters but is free to focus on preaching, teaching, and interceding for the congregation.

It is important to note that biblically the deacon is not a church ruler or a supervisor over the pastor. Deacons are servants of the Body of Christ, helpers of the pastor, and ministers to the people.

Question Four: What Is the Ministry of Trustees?

Geoffrey V. Guns, in his book Spiritual Leadership: A Guide to Developing Spiritual Leaders in the Church, teaches that trustees serve as the legal representatives of the church. Their responsibilities include holding the title and deed to church property, signing legal documents related to the purchase, sale, mortgage, or rental of church property, assisting with the upkeep of the church facilities, and working with the treasurer and financial secretary to ensure financial stability—all under the leadership of the pastor.

Dr. Guns also emphasizes the importance of understanding state law. In Virginia, for example, the laws governing church trustees are clearly defined (Code of Virginia 57-8; 57-9; 57-12; 8.01-220.1:1). These laws establish the trustee role as the legal representative of the congregation in matters of property and finance.

From a biblical perspective, trustees are also stewards. Matthew 25:14-28 reminds us of the importance of faithful stewardship. Trustees are charged with handling the church's resources responsibly, not for personal gain, but for the advancement of God's Kingdom. Their ministry is one of service and accountability, ensuring that the church's physical and financial resources are used to glorify God.

Question Five: What Is the Ministry of the Associate Minister?

There is a common misconception that the call to ministry always equals a call to preach. K. Edward Copeland, in his book Riding in the Second Chariot: A Guide for Associate Ministers, points out that not every call to ministry is a preaching call. Even when the call involves preaching, it does not necessarily mean one will be called to be a pastor.

Unfortunately, many pastors and churches rush to license individuals without discerning their true gifts and calling. This is a mistake. It is the pastor's responsibility, with the help of church leadership, to ensure that anyone seeking licensure is properly examined and prepared. Paul warned against laying hands on individuals too quickly (I Tim. 5:22). Proper training, preparation, and discernment are necessary before sending anyone forth into ministry.

The late pastor of Eighth Street Baptist Church in Lynchburg, Virginia, once said, "The call to preach is a call to preparation." Jesus modeled this by training His disciples before sending them out (Matt. 5–7). Copeland also noted that genuine preachers have an irresistible urge to study and proclaim God's Word (II Tim. 2:15). Those who resist training or avoid

230

preparation reveal that they are not truly called to the preaching ministry.

Associate ministers should also be guided by wisdom and humility. They must ensure that their families support their call, spend quality time with their loved ones, and respect their pastor's leadership. They should never undermine their pastor, but rather pray for him, support him, and encourage the congregation to follow his leadership. Associate ministers must avoid imitating others and instead develop their own voice. They should wait patiently for opportunities to preach, participate actively in the ministries of the church, and serve faithfully when called upon.

A Final Word

Deacons, trustees, and associate ministers must never forget that titles do not make leaders—true leaders make the title meaningful. A servant's heart, a commitment to prayer, a spirit of humility, and a willingness to work together under the pastor's leadership are the marks of Kingdom service. When these roles are embraced with integrity and dedication, the church becomes stronger, healthier, and more effective in fulfilling the mission of Jesus Christ.

Lesson 47
Notes on Tithes and Offerings

Scripture: Malachi 3:8-10

The Origin of Tithing

Tithing began in the Old Testament as a direct commandment from God. It was both an act of obedience and a demonstration of Israel's faith in God as their provider. The very first recorded example of tithing is found in Genesis 14. After Abraham rescued his nephew Lot and won a great victory over his enemies, he encountered Melchizedek, the king of Salem and priest of God. Out of gratitude and reverence, Abraham gave Melchizedek a tithe, or one-tenth, of everything he had obtained in battle (Genesis 14:17-20). This sets the biblical precedent that tithing is not merely a human idea but a God-ordained practice of worship and acknowledgement of His provision.

The Purpose of Tithing in the Old Testament

According to Old Testament scholars, the tithe had several purposes beyond simply being a religious ritual. First, it was intended to support the Levites, who had no land inheritance and were devoted to temple service. It was also used to care for the stranger, the fatherless, and the widow (Deuteronomy 26:12-13).

This reveals that tithing was not only an act of worship but also a means of social justice and compassion. It ensured that God's people cared for the vulnerable among them.

Tithing also expressed gratitude. By giving the first tenth, Israel acknowledged that everything belonged to God. As Psalm 24:1-2 reminds us, "The earth is the Lord's, and the fullness thereof; the world, and they that dwell therein." Tithing was a way for the people to confess that God was the true owner of all their blessings and that they were merely stewards.

Tithing as God's Financial Plan for the Church

Tithing is not just an Old Testament practice; it remains God's financial plan for His church today. To tithe is to return ten percent of your earnings back to God, allowing the church to function and the work of ministry to continue. Jesus Himself emphasized that God must always be first in our lives when He said, "Seek ye first the kingdom of God and his righteousness; and all these things shall be added unto you" (Matthew 6:33).

Tithing is a discipline that teaches believers to put God first in their finances and to trust Him for provision. It is not about what God needs but about shaping the heart of the giver to live in obedience and dependence on Him.

Tithing Is the Fairest Way to Give

One of the remarkable aspects of tithing is its fairness. The tithe is always ten percent, no matter the size of your income. This means that everyone gives the same portion, though not the same dollar amount. Deuteronomy 16:17 teaches that, "Every man shall give as he is able, according to the blessings of the Lord thy God which he hath given thee."

This means that someone with more income may give more dollars, but both the wealthy and the poor give equally in proportion to what God has blessed them with. In this way, no one is left out, and no one carries a greater burden than another. Tithing unites the entire congregation in shared responsibility and obedience, as everyone participates according to their ability.

Robbing God or Trusting God?

Malachi 3:8-10 addresses a sobering reality about tithing. When God's people withhold their tithes and offerings, He says they are "robbing God." In Malachi's time, Israel was guilty of bringing only part of their tithes to the temple while keeping the rest for themselves. Their disobedience revealed a self-centered heart that placed personal desires above God's commands. By holding back, they were misusing what rightly belonged to God.

The consequences were severe. Malachi 3:9 states that those who refuse to tithe are "cursed with a curse," highlighting that disobedience brings negative consequences both spiritually and materially. However, the opposite is also true. Malachi 3:10 contains one of God's greatest promises: when His people bring the whole tithe into the storehouse, He will "open the windows of heaven" and pour out blessings beyond measure. The choice is clear: robbing God leads to loss, but trusting God leads to overflowing provision.

Friendly Advice: Do not be guilty of robbing God for selfish gain or personal pleasure. Instead, take God at His Word and trust Him with your giving.

A Practical Guide to Tithing

Many people struggle with the concept of tithing because they wonder if they can afford it. The truth is, tithing is an act of faith. It requires believing that God can sustain you better on ninety percent of your income than you can sustain yourself on one hundred percent.

To help you begin, consider the chart. It provides a simple example of how much a tithe would be based on weekly income. This chart shows that no matter the amount of income, the principle of ten percent remains consistent.

Weekly Income	Tithes
$40.00	$4.00
$50.00	$5.00
$60.00	$6.00
$70.00	$7.00
$80.00	$8.00
$90.00	$9.00
$100.00	$10.00
$200.00	$20.00
$300.00	$30.00
$400.00	$40.00
$500.00	$50.00

This simple guide reminds us that tithing is not complicated. It is a consistent discipline that keeps our hearts aligned with God's will.

Final Word

Tithing and giving offerings are not about money alone. They are about faith, obedience, and trust in God. When we give, we are not simply handing over a portion of our income; we are declaring with our actions that God is the true source of everything we have. Malachi 3:10 reminds us that God challenges His people to test Him in this area. It is one of the few times in Scripture where God invites us to prove His faithfulness, and His promise is clear: if we obey, He will open the windows of heaven and pour out blessings we cannot contain.

When we choose to tithe faithfully, we shift our focus from fear of lack to confidence in God's provision. The discipline of giving teaches us to live with open hands, releasing selfishness and materialism while embracing gratitude and stewardship. It reminds us that everything we have is on loan from God, and we are merely stewards of His resources. In this way, tithing becomes an act of worship, a declaration that God is first in our lives, even in the area of finances.

Take a step of faith today and begin where you are. Trust God to supply your needs and honor His Word with your tithe. As you do, you will quickly discover that life is richer, fuller, and more blessed when you put God first. He has promised that you can live better on ninety percent with His blessing than on one hundred percent without it. The joy and peace that come from obedience will strengthen your faith and remind you daily that God is faithful to those who trust Him.

Lesson 48
Responsibilities of Church Members to their Pastor

Scripture: I Corinthians 9:11-14

A church has several key responsibilities toward its pastor. These responsibilities include financial support, spiritual care, prayer, and demonstrating respect. When these are practiced faithfully, the pastor can lead effectively and serve the congregation without unnecessary burdens. A pastor is called to shepherd God's people, but the success of their ministry also depends on the cooperation and support of those they lead. By understanding and fulfilling their responsibilities, church members play a vital role in building up the body of Christ and advancing the Kingdom of God.

Responsibility 1: Appreciate Your Pastor (1 Thessalonians 5:12-13)

The first responsibility of church members is to appreciate and respect their pastor. The Thessalonian believers were instructed to recognize those who diligently labored among them, thanking God for their willingness to pour themselves out physically, mentally, and emotionally for the church. To appreciate your pastor is more than just words; it is acknowledging their hard work and sacrifice. Paul makes it clear that pastors are those who have charge over you, meaning they have a God-given authority to lead, protect, and care for the flock. They admonish, warn, and correct those in error to strengthen the church. Members demonstrate appreciation when they honor this role, showing gratitude for the pastor's labor of love.

Responsibility 2: Esteem Your Pastor (1 Thessalonians 5:12-13)

Beyond appreciation, members are also called to esteem their pastors. To esteem means to hold in high regard, to value them because of the sacred work they do. Ministry is not an ordinary job but a high and holy calling. Church members must place proper value on the pastoral office, treating their leaders with dignity and respect. This is not about elevating the person above others but recognizing the weight of their responsibility before God. When a church esteems its pastor, it creates a culture of honor where ministry flourishes, and the congregation benefits from the encouragement and stability such respect brings.

Responsibility 3: Obey Your Pastor (Hebrews 13:17)

Obedience is another essential responsibility. To obey in this context means to listen attentively and be persuaded by the pastor's leadership as it aligns with Scripture. This is not a blind or cult-like allegiance, but a trust that stems from confidence in their God-given ability to lead. Pastors are accountable before God for how they shepherd His people, and members are accountable for how they respond to that leadership. When the church body follows the biblical guidance and instruction of its pastor, unity is strengthened, and the work of ministry becomes more effective. Obedience is a practical way of supporting pastoral leadership.

Responsibility 4: Submit to Your Pastor (Hebrews 13:17)

Closely tied to obedience is the responsibility of submission. Submission goes beyond outward compliance; it is a matter of the heart. To submit is to yield willingly and cheerfully to pastoral leadership, recognizing that pastors are charged with watching over the souls of the congregation. This responsibility is compared to that of a guard or watchman who remains alert to protect from danger. Just as the Coast Guard warns of storms or an air traffic controller keeps watch for collisions, pastors remain spiritually alert to warn God's people of subtle dangers and errors. When members submit to this oversight, they are protecting their own spiritual welfare.

240

Responsibility 5: Support Your Pastor (1 Timothy 5:17-18)

Support involves both respect and financial provision. Paul is clear that those who labor in teaching and preaching are worthy of "double honor," meaning they deserve both respect and material support. Just as an ox was not to be muzzled while threshing grain, pastors must be free to live from the gospel without being hindered by financial struggles. When a church fails to provide adequately for its pastor and their family, it hinders their ability to minister effectively. Supporting your pastor ensures that they can devote themselves fully to prayer, study, and shepherding the congregation without distraction.

Responsibility 6: Discipline Your Pastor When It Is Needed (1 Timothy 5:19-20)

While pastors deserve appreciation, esteem, obedience, submission, and support, they must also be held accountable. Discipline is necessary when a pastor is guilty of open sin or serious doctrinal error. Paul instructed Timothy that accusations against leaders must be handled carefully, requiring two or three witnesses to establish the truth. This safeguard protects pastors from false or malicious charges while also ensuring accountability. When sin or error is proven, the church must act in love and truth to correct and discipline. True love for God and for spiritual leaders means being willing to protect the integrity of the church, even when discipline is difficult.

Responsibility 7: Remember Your Pastor (Hebrews 13:7)

To remember your pastor means to call them to mind continually, not forgetting the weight of their responsibility or the sacrifices they make. This responsibility is best expressed through prayer. The congregation must intercede for their pastor regularly, knowing that Satan targets spiritual leaders to scatter the flock. Prayer strengthens and protects pastors in their ministry. Remembering also involves encouragement, kind words, and practical acts of support. When members actively remember their pastor, they create an environment where the leader is strengthened and the church flourishes under God's guidance.

Responsibility 8: Mimic Your Pastor (Hebrews 13:7)

Finally, church members are instructed to mimic or imitate their pastor's faith. God gave qualifications for pastoral leadership so that His people would have visible role models to follow. Paul declared, "Be imitators of me, just as I also am of Christ" (1 Cor. 11:1). This was not arrogance but confidence that he was faithfully following Christ in his own life. Members who imitate the godly lives of their pastors demonstrate the transforming power of the gospel to the world. When the congregation mirrors the example of their leaders, they reproduce faithfulness, obedience, and love, and the gospel is advanced in visible, powerful ways.

Final Word

The responsibilities of church members to their pastor are not optional suggestions; they are biblical commands that strengthen the life of the church. When members appreciate, esteem, obey, submit, support, and remember their pastor, they create an environment where ministry thrives, unity is protected, and the gospel advances with power.

A faithful pastor gives their life in prayer, study, teaching, and shepherding. In return, the congregation is called to provide encouragement, accountability, and tangible support so that the pastor can serve with joy and not with grief. When both pastor and congregation walk in obedience to their God-given roles, the church becomes a true reflection of Christ's love and order.

As Paul reminded the Corinthians, "the Lord ordained that those who preach the gospel should live from the gospel" (1 Cor. 9:14). Let us therefore remember our pastors, lift them in prayer, encourage them with words and actions, and follow their example as they follow Christ. In doing so, we not only bless our leaders but also glorify God and strengthen His church for Kingdom service.

Lesson 49
Pastor Search Committee

Scripture: Jeremiah 3:14 and I Corinthians 14:40

Why a Pastor Search Committee?

One of the most important decisions in the life of a church is selecting a pastor. The pastor is the spiritual shepherd and leader, and the future health of the congregation depends greatly on this decision. Sadly, many good churches have been hijacked by misleading, deceitful, and dishonest individuals posing as men or women of God. This has caused division, mistrust, and even destruction in congregations that failed to take the process seriously. The only foolproof way to avoid such a tragedy is to ensure that the leadership, members, and the pulpit committee are fully in touch with the Lord throughout the process. Those selected to serve on the Pastor Search Committee must be spiritually mature, word-centered, and prayerful individuals who can discern the will of God rather than be swayed by personal opinions or preferences.

What is a Pastor Search Committee?

A Pastor Search Committee, sometimes called a Pastoral/Search Committee, is a group of carefully selected church members assigned the responsibility of seeking out suitable pastoral candidates. Their role is to recommend qualified individuals to the congregation for consideration and possible election as pastor. In most cases, this committee should be relatively small, usually between five and seven members, depending on the size of the church. The smaller size allows for efficient communication, confidentiality, and focus, while still representing the voice of the congregation. This committee becomes one of the most critical temporary ministries of the church, as its decisions will affect the entire congregation for years to come.

How Many Members Should Serve on the Pastor Search Committee?

The size of the committee can either help or hinder the search process. The adage, "Too many cooks in the kitchen," applies here. Too many members often leads to unnecessary confusion, division, and delays, while too few members risk underrepresentation of the congregation's diverse views. The goal is to find a balance. A committee of five to seven individuals provides enough diversity of thought without creating excessive conflict or slowing the process. When structured properly, each member will feel valued, and the church will trust that their voices are represented.

What Should the Church Do When the Pulpit Becomes Vacant?

When a pulpit becomes vacant, whether through the death, retirement, resignation, or dismissal of a pastor, the church must respond with order and prayer. Several steps can be taken to ensure stability during the transition.

First, the Diaconate Ministry may be empowered to oversee the church's affairs temporarily. Their role should be limited to oversight and not dictation, ensuring that the church continues to function until a new pastor is elected.

Second, the church should hold a regular or specially called meeting to select a Pastor Search Committee. This committee is responsible for inviting ministers to conduct worship services, filling the pulpit as needed until a permanent pastor is chosen. The committee operates under the authority of the church and must report back at every business meeting. Their work must always be done under the careful watch of the church body. To ensure balance, the committee should reflect the fabric of the congregation, including representatives from various ministries such as the Diaconate, Trustees, Youth, Music, and Christian Education.

The committee must also have a Chairman and a Secretary. The Chairman's role is not to dictate decisions, but to preside over meetings and provide reports to the church as required. The Secretary is responsible for keeping accurate minutes of all meetings, maintaining records of invited ministers, and organizing correspondence. Importantly, the committee must remain open to suggestions from church members and never attempt to impose its personal preferences on the congregation. If any member disrupts the process or causes chaos, the church has the right to remove that member or, if necessary, dissolve the entire committee and appoint a new one.

Third, the church may choose to select an Interim Pastor during a business meeting to provide consistent leadership until a permanent pastor is elected.

Fourth, if available, the Assistant Pastor or Associate Ministers may be asked to conduct services until the Pastor Search Committee is fully formed and empowered to move forward.

The weight of this decision cannot be overstated. The selection of a pastor is both a great privilege and a great responsibility. For this reason, the church family must commit to praying continually for the committee, asking the Holy Spirit to guide every decision and reveal the person whom God has chosen.

First Things First

Before the search process begins, both the church and the committee must come together in prayer. This spiritual foundation is crucial to ensure that the selection is aligned with God's will. The first practical step is to identify the needs of both the church and the surrounding community. A pastor must not only preach and teach but also be equipped to address the unique needs of the congregation and its context.

The church must then carefully determine what type of pastor is required. Some congregations need a strong preacher, while others need a teacher-preacher combination. Still others may need an organizer, a visionary leader, or someone with experience in church growth or education. The needs of the church should drive the type of leader they seek. Once these needs are identified, the committee should seek resumes from multiple sources, including seminaries, Bible colleges, state conventions, ministerial fellowships, church members, and other pastors. These resumes should then be prayerfully and carefully reviewed to ensure that only those who meet the church's needs and align with its vision are considered.

Things to Consider When Reviewing Resumes

When reviewing resumes, the committee must look beyond appearances. The first question should be whether the candidate has the skills and experience needed for the church's unique situation. Secondly, the resume itself should reflect the candidate's ability to communicate clearly and concisely, since communication is a key part of pastoral ministry. Thirdly, the committee should carefully consider the candidate's past ministry experiences, whether volunteer, part-time, or full-time. Every experience shapes the leader's ability to serve, and these should not be overlooked. Finally, the educational background of the candidate should be weighed against the needs of the church. Not all degrees or institutions carry the same weight, and not every church requires the same educational credentials. Discernment is required to determine whether the candidate's preparation matches the church's expectations.

Members of the Pastor Search Committee Must...

Effective Pastor Search Committees share five critical qualities.

They must be humble. Humility ensures that the members pursue God's will instead of personal agendas. They must remember that their responsibility is not to find a pastor who fits their personal preference, but one who fulfills God's call for the church.

They must be prayerful. A praying committee is a powerful committee. Prayer is not an afterthought but the foundation of the entire process. From the first meeting to the final recommendation, every step should be bathed in prayer.

They must be patient. Rushing the process often leads to mistakes and regrets. The biggest error many committees make is becoming anxious and appointing the wrong leader because they did not wait on the

Lord's timing. Patience ensures that the decision is deliberate and Spirit-led.

They must be intentional. Planning the work and working the plan allows the committee to stay focused. This involves setting timelines, assigning responsibilities, and being organized throughout the process.

Finally, they must be thorough. Every "i" must be dotted and every "t" crossed. This means checking references, verifying education and experience, and asking difficult questions when necessary. A thorough process demonstrates respect for both the church and the candidate.

Final Word

The Pastor Search Committee holds one of the most sacred and serious responsibilities in the life of the church. By being humble, prayerful, patient, intentional, and thorough, they can fulfill their calling and present to the church the leader whom God has already prepared. When the process is done in order and under the guidance of the Holy Spirit, the congregation can move forward with confidence, knowing that they have sought God's will and chosen a shepherd to lead them in Kingdom service.

Lesson 50
Church Leadership: Teaming Together to Do Ministry

Scripture: Luke 10:1; I Corinthians 14:40

John C. Maxwell once said, "True leadership must be for the benefit of the followers, not to enrich the leader." This principle captures the very heart of biblical leadership within the church. From both the Old and New Testaments, we learn that God has always identified and raised spiritual leaders to oversee His people. In the church today, the pastor is the one entrusted with this sacred role. Scripture describes the pastor as the overseer, leader, and administrator of the local church (Jeremiah 3:15; Acts 20:28; Ephesians 4:11-13). In essence, the pastor functions as the spiritual Chief Executive Officer of the congregation, responsible for overseeing every entity and guiding the church to function in unity, order, and purpose.

The Pastor's Administrative Responsibilities

Every officer, leader, and worker in the church ultimately serves under the authority of the pastor. Nothing in the church should be done without the pastor's knowledge or approval, because God has placed the pastor as the overseer of the local body. The pastor is responsible for overseeing worship, ensuring

251

that ordinances are observed, guiding the administration, managing the church's finances, caring for membership, and supervising all ministries and auxiliaries. Everything the church is involved in, from the smallest detail to the largest undertaking, ultimately falls under the pastor's responsibility.

It is a mistake to think of the pastor as only someone who preaches on Sundays, teaches Bible study, officiates weddings, or visits the sick. While these are important duties, the pastor's role is far greater. The pastor is both a spiritual leader and an administrator, ensuring that the church functions decently and in order. This broader responsibility means that pastors must be supported in their work and respected as God's appointed leaders for the church.

The Difference Between Early Church Leaders and Today's Leaders

In Matthew 5 through 7, Jesus trained His disciples thoroughly before releasing them to assist Him in ministry. The early church leaders were willing to be taught and understood the necessity of spiritual preparation (Matthew 5:1-2). By contrast, in many churches today, leaders, including pastors, deacons, and other officers, resist training or fail to see its importance. This creates a dangerous gap in servant leadership.

When leaders are trained in the biblical model of servant leadership, their focus shifts from ruling and controlling to serving and equipping others. The Apostle Paul reminded Timothy of the importance of study and preparation so that ministry could be carried out without shame (II Timothy 2:15). Leaders who neglect training often fall into patterns of pride or authoritarianism, but those who embrace learning embody humility and servanthood.

The 21st Century Church Is in Need of Servant Leaders

The modern church desperately needs leaders who are firmly grounded in God's Word, obedient to both God and the local pastor, and filled with love for the Lord, the church, and His people. Servant leaders seek to please God rather than themselves, and they will not compromise with the devil for personal gain or influence.

Leadership must not be defined by rank, status, fame, or personality. Jesus addressed this clearly in Matthew 20:25-28 when His disciples became upset over a request for special authority. Jesus explained that while worldly rulers seek to dominate and exercise authority, the true measure of greatness in God's Kingdom is found in servanthood. He Himself modeled this by declaring that He came not to be served, but to serve and to give His life as a ransom for many. According to Jesus, leadership is not about self-promotion but about sacrifice, service, and humility. Leaders who follow His example will lead with unselfish hearts, while those who seek power and recognition will fall short of His standard.

The Purpose of Church Administration

Charles Tidwell, in his book Church Administration: Effective Leadership, explained that church administration is leadership that equips the church to be the church and to do the work of the church. Manuel Scott, the late renowned preacher, echoed this truth by declaring, "Let the church be the church." The Apostle Paul also emphasized that leadership within the church must always be carried out decently and in order (I Corinthians 14:40).

Church administration is not merely about paperwork, schedules, and meetings. It involves the careful use of the church's spiritual, human, physical, and financial resources to fulfill its God-given mission. When done properly, administration becomes a ministry in itself—guiding the church in worship, service, discipleship, and evangelism while ensuring that all parts of the body function together in harmony.

Church Vision and Mission Statements

Every church should have a vision and mission statement to guide its direction and clarify its purpose. The vision statement articulates the church's ambition, presenting a clear and concise picture of the desired change that results from its ministry. The mission statement, on the other hand, explains why the church exists. It describes its purpose, intentions, and objectives, providing a framework for action.

For example, a church vision might be stated as: "Our vision is to reach, connect, and serve a multigenerational and multicultural group for Jesus Christ." The corresponding mission might read: "Our mission is to be the church that displays the love of Christ and connects with people of all walks of life through our creative services, discipleship, and outreach." A strong mission statement must answer the question: How will the church make the vision a reality? When practiced, it creates unity and gives the church a common purpose.

Team Leadership Within the Church

Good church administration must be paired with team leadership. Team leadership is the collective work of believers who unite under the oversight of the pastor to fulfill the mission of the church. This includes official staff, hired staff, volunteer workers, and the congregation working side by side as servant-leaders. The purpose is to expand the ministries of the church,

255

meet the needs of the membership, and evangelize the unsaved.

Even Jesus did not do ministry alone. According to Mark 3:13-19 and Luke 6:12-16, He selected twelve apostles to assist Him in His work. This model of teamwork is essential for the church today. Unfortunately, too often, pastors, deacons, trustees, or individual members attempt to carry out ministry alone, which almost always results in conflict and division. Healthy team leadership ensures that no one carries the burden alone and that all gifts are used for God's glory.

Members of the leadership team must be gifted with talents, leadership abilities, and administrative skills to help the church grow. The head of the church leadership team is the pastor, not the deacons, trustees, clerks, or any other individuals. The mission of the team is to please God, not themselves. The early church demonstrated this on the day of Pentecost, when they pleased God and were filled with the Spirit, and the Lord added to their numbers daily (Acts 2:47).

For this teamwork to be effective, every leader must stay in their lane. Each team member should have a written job description and be held accountable for fulfilling their responsibilities without interfering with the duties of others. Deacons should not interfere with the pastor's responsibilities, trustees should not interfere with deacons, and clerks should not interfere with Christian Education. When every leader stays in their lane, the church functions smoothly.

Church Administration and Organization

Tidwell defined organization as "the arrangement of persons to get the job done." Every church should have an organizational chart and written job descriptions for its leaders. A good organization distributes the workload, ensuring that no one person carries all the responsibility. It places accountability where it belongs, and it reduces confusion. An organizational chart is a simple but powerful way to visualize who does what and who reports to whom in the church.

A vital part of leadership is delegation. A pastor cannot do everything alone, nor should they try. Effective delegation ensures that responsibilities are shared, and the church functions efficiently. Jesus modeled this when He fed the 5,000. He did not do it alone but entrusted His disciples to distribute the food (John 6:1-14). This demonstrates the power of teamwork and delegation in ministry.

Ministry Leaders' Responsibilities in a Nutshell

Each ministry leader within the church has distinct responsibilities. Deacons assist the pastor with the spiritual affairs, ministries, and administration of the church. Trustees handle the legal and financial affairs, ensuring that the church remains solvent and the property is well-maintained. Clerks or secretaries keep accurate records of minutes, membership, and church correspondence, while treasurers and financial

257

secretaries safeguard and manage the church's finances. Ministers of music and musicians provide worship through song and music. Youth directors disciple young people, shaping their faith and biblical worldview. Sunday School Superintendents oversee Christian education, and presidents of various ministries guide their groups, keep members engaged, and report back to the pastor and officers.

Final Word

True leadership in the church is not about titles, recognition, or power. It is about serving God and His people with humility, sacrifice, and love. Titles do not make leaders; instead, leaders make titles by how they serve and model Christ to others. Every church leader must guard against pride and remember that leadership is a call to servanthood. When the church embraces this model of teaming together to do ministry, it will fulfill its mission, build up the body of Christ, and bring glory to God.

Lesson 51
Bullying in the Church

Scripture: Matthew 5:44; Ephesians 4:29-31

Bullying is often thought of as a problem confined to public schools, college campuses, or workplace settings, but the truth is that it occurs in every environment, from the poorhouse to the White House—including the church. Week after week, in churches across the globe, people experience bullying at the hands of church officials, members, or even entire groups. This reality makes bullying in the church a serious issue that must be acknowledged and addressed directly. When left unchecked, it can wound individuals deeply, damage the unity of the congregation, and ultimately hinder the witness of the church in the world.

What Is Bullying?

Bullying can be defined as repeated, intentional behavior where someone says or does hurtful and mean things to another person to cause harm. It is not a one-time disagreement or conflict but rather a pattern of behavior meant to intimidate, belittle, or dominate someone else.

259

A bully, therefore, is a quarrelsome, overbearing individual who uses intimidation, manipulation, or badgering to assert power over others. In the context of the church, this could be a member who constantly criticizes and embarrasses others, a leader who misuses authority to control, or even groups of people who exclude or mistreat individuals they deem unworthy.

Four Types of Bullying

Researchers who study bullying generally identify four categories of bullying. The first is physical bullying, which includes harmful actions such as hitting, kicking, spitting, tripping, pushing, breaking personal belongings, or making rude physical gestures. The second is verbal bullying, where words are used as weapons through teasing, name-calling, threats, inappropriate sexual comments, or taunting. The third is social bullying, which is often more subtle but equally damaging. This includes deliberately excluding someone from a group, spreading rumors, embarrassing them publicly, or convincing others not to associate with them. Finally, there is cyberbullying, which has become increasingly common in recent years. This involves harassing or humiliating someone through electronic means such as texting, emails, or posts on social media platforms. Unfortunately, even in the church, all four types can take place when love and accountability are absent.

Lesson 1: Love Is the Ultimate Remedy for Bullying in the Church

The ultimate antidote to bullying is found in the command of Jesus Christ to love one another. In Mark 12 and Luke 6, Jesus reminds us to love our neighbors as ourselves and to treat others in the same way we would want to be treated (Mark 12:30-31; Luke 6:31). When this command becomes the guiding principle of a congregation, bullying cannot thrive. Love builds up instead of tearing down, and it heals instead of wounding. It calls believers to see others as children of God, worthy of respect, dignity, and compassion. When love becomes the standard in both words and actions, the toxic power of bullying is broken.

Lesson 2: Church Bullying Is Never Okay

Bullying of any kind contradicts the essence of the Christian faith. Every person, regardless of their background, personality, or appearance, has been created in the image of God (Genesis 1:26-27). To demean or belittle another person is to dishonor the image of God in them. The Book of James warns against using our tongues for both blessing and cursing, reminding us that such behavior is inconsistent for followers of Christ (James 3:1-10, 16). The Apostle Paul also admonishes believers to let no corrupt communication come out of their mouths, but only that which builds up and ministers grace (Ephesians 4:29). When church members engage in bullying through gossip, insults, or exclusion, they dishonor God and harm the body of Christ. True Christianity calls for speech and behavior that reflect godliness, not foulness or abuse.

Lesson 3: Church Bullying Is Not a New Problem Among Believers

While bullying in the church may feel like a modern problem, it is not new. Scripture reveals that God's people have always faced mistreatment from others. Ecclesiastes 1:9 reminds us that there is nothing new under the sun, and bullying is no exception. From the earliest stories of the Bible, we see people targeting others with cruelty, envy, and intimidation.

For example, Cain bullied his brother Abel and ultimately killed him out of jealousy (Genesis 4:8). Joseph's brothers mocked, stripped, and cast him into a pit before selling him into slavery (Genesis 37:23-24). Nehemiah faced ridicule and opposition from Sanballat, Tobiah, and Geshem as they tried to hinder his work of rebuilding Jerusalem's wall (Nehemiah 2:19). Shadrach, Meshach, and Abednego were bullied by King Nebuchadnezzar, who threatened them with death for refusing to bow to his idol (Daniel 3:15). Goliath openly mocked and bullied young David, trying to intimidate him before battle (1 Samuel 17:42-51). Even the early church was bullied, as Saul persecuted and scattered believers (Acts 8:1-4).

Jesus Was Bullied During His Life on Earth

Even our Lord Jesus Christ experienced bullying. After His birth, King Herod attempted to kill Him out of fear and jealousy (Matthew 2:16). Following His baptism, Satan sought to bully Him with temptations and taunts (Matthew 4:3, 6, 9). Later, during His ministry, religious leaders bullied Him with mockery, false accusations, and violent opposition, especially during His arrest and trial (Matthew 26:55-68). Jesus knows firsthand what it means to be the target of bullying, and His life shows us how to endure it with grace and steadfastness.

Final Word

The church is called to be a place of refuge, love, and healing. It's not a place of bullying. When bullying is present within the church, it distorts the message of the gospel and wounds the very people Christ came to save. Leaders and members alike must commit themselves to treating one another with love, kindness, and respect, as Scripture teaches (1 Peter 2:21-23). Believers are called to pray for one another, support one another, and walk together in unity. By confronting bullying and choosing to love instead, the church can truly become a reflection of Christ's Kingdom on earth, where every individual is valued, protected, and nurtured in the love of God.

Lesson 52
The Church and Prayer

Scripture: Acts 4:31-32; Acts 12:5

Growing up in the church, I often witnessed God moving in powerful ways. I saw lives changed, burdens lifted, and the Holy Spirit working among the people. I found myself asking the question: Where did the church get its power? As I studied the New Testament Book of Acts and explored church history, I came to an important realization. The church did not receive its power from the singing of the choir, no matter how beautiful or inspiring the music might have been. The power did not come from the service of the Diaconate or the Trustees, as faithful as they were in their duties. Neither did it come solely from the preaching of the pastor, no matter how gifted the sermon might have been. Instead, the true power of the church came from prayer directed to God and answered by the Holy Spirit.

Throughout the Bible, we see that the outpouring of the Holy Spirit was never random or coincidental. It came when God's people prayed. A powerful example of this is found in Acts 12, which records the church praying for Peter while he was in prison awaiting execution. Verse 5 tells us that the church prayed without ceasing for him. Their persistence in prayer moved the hand of God, who not only heard them but answered. In verses 7 through 16, we read of Peter's miraculous release, proving that the prayers of God's people can change situations that seem impossible.

The lesson is clear: history shows that every great movement of God can be traced back to men and women who prayed. The presence of God, I believe, is not experienced in empty rituals, empty buildings, or empty hearts. His presence is revealed in people who gather in His name with sincere and fervent prayer.

Lesson I: The Church Must Pray in Unity

One of the greatest strengths of the early church was its unity in prayer. Acts 4 tells us that the believers were of one heart and one soul, praying and seeking God together (Acts 4:32). Their prayers were not limited to the Apostles; the entire body of believers joined in intercession. Unity in prayer created a spiritual atmosphere where the power of God could freely move. David declared in Psalm 133:1 that it is both good and pleasant when brethren dwell together in unity, and the early church modeled this principle in action.

When the church unites in prayer today, the same results can be experienced. The presence of God will fill the congregation, and the power of the Holy Spirit will be evident. Leaders and members alike must set aside personal agendas, differences, and distractions, coming together as one body to seek God's face. When prayer is united, it becomes unstoppable, and the church is positioned to experience revival.

Lesson II: When the Church Prays, the Power of God Is Received

The Day of Pentecost in Acts 2 is a prime example of what happens when the church prays. The believers gathered in the upper room with one accord, continually devoting themselves to prayer (Acts 1:14). As they prayed, the Holy Spirit was poured out upon every person in that place (Acts 2:1-4). The power they received enabled them to do exactly what Jesus had commanded them to do.

First, they spoke in languages that allowed the message of the gospel to be understood by people from many different nations. This miracle of communication broke down barriers and showed that the gospel was for everyone. Second, they boldly evangelized and witnessed throughout the known world, beginning immediately in Jerusalem and spreading outward. Third, they developed deep fellowship, eating, worshipping, and praising God together with glad hearts (Acts 4:31).

This pattern shows us that prayer is the key that unlocks the power of the Holy Spirit in the church. When a local congregation devotes itself to prayer, it is empowered to bless its community, strengthen its members, and proclaim God's Word with boldness. Without prayer, the church becomes weak, but with prayer, it becomes a vessel of divine power.

Lesson III: When the Church Prays, the Purpose of God Is Achieved

Another important outcome of prayer is that the church is enabled to fulfill the purpose of God. Acts 4:29-32 describes believers speaking the Word of God with boldness, and this boldness characterized their entire ministry. In the New Testament, the word "boldness" carries three important ideas.

First, it means having the courage to speak, even in the face of opposition or fear. The early church did not remain silent about the gospel, even though they faced threats and persecution. Second, boldness refers to the ability to communicate the message of Jesus clearly and plainly. The church was not vague or hesitant in its proclamation but spoke in a way that people could understand. Third, boldness carries the sense of confidence in what is being spoken. The believers did not wonder whether the gospel was true; they knew it, believed it, and declared it without shame.

For the church today, the same principles apply. If we are to grow and fulfill God's mission, leaders and members must devote themselves to prayer. We must pray for God's will to be made known, for His power to be manifest, for souls to be saved, and for the church to expand. Prayer aligns the church with God's purpose and ensures that His kingdom work is carried out effectively.

Final Word

The connection between prayer and power cannot be overstated. As the saying goes: little prayer, little power; some prayer, some power; much prayer, much power; no prayer, no power. The church's ability to impact the world depends directly on its willingness to pray. Without prayer, the church loses its strength, its direction, and its effectiveness. But with prayer, the church becomes a powerful instrument in the hands of God, capable of transforming lives and communities.

Prayer is not an optional activity. It is the lifeline of the church. If we long to see revival, growth, and the movement of the Holy Spirit, we must recommit ourselves to prayer, both individually and collectively. Only then will the church truly reflect the power, presence, and purpose of God in the world.

Lesson 53
Don't Be Guilty of Doing Ministry for the Wrong Reasons

Scripture: Matthew 6:1; Ephesians 6:6

Ministry is not meant to be a performance. It is not a platform for personal validation, nor is it a stage for gaining power, praise, or position. Ministry is a sacred calling, a divine opportunity to serve God by serving others. Yet the sobering truth is that many believers, and even leaders, fall into the dangerous trap of doing ministry for the wrong reasons. When motives are impure, ministry loses its integrity. God not only looks at what we do, but also at why we do it. He weighs the heart. And when our hearts are not right, even good works can become misaligned with His purpose.

The Danger of Wrong Motives in Ministry

It is entirely possible to be active in ministry yet be completely out of step with God's will. One can be busy with church work while at the same time neglecting the heart of Christ's work. When this happens, ministry becomes burdensome, bitter, and broken. Jesus warned His disciples in Matthew 6 not to perform righteous acts simply to be seen by others. The Pharisees were guilty of this, giving loudly, fasting publicly, and praying with carefully crafted words just to impress those around them. Jesus made it clear: if the reward you seek is applause, then applause is all you will receive. There will be no reward from the Father in heaven.

Examining the Heart Behind Service

Why do you serve? Why do you preach, teach, usher, sing, give, or lead? If the answer is recognition, reputation, influence, or affirmation, then the reward has already been given in the form of human praise. But if the service flows from love, humility, and obedience to God, then the reward is eternal. The Apostle Paul urged believers not to serve as "men-pleasers," but as "servants of Christ." This means that our motivation must be anchored in a desire to please God, even when the work is difficult, unnoticed, or costly.

Serving for the wrong reasons can lead to burnout. It makes ministry into a competition rather than a calling. It turns the platform into a place of pride instead of purpose. It shifts relationships into rivalries and makes leaders into dictators. This is not the heart of Christ. Jesus modeled true ministry when He humbled Himself to wash the disciples' feet. The Son of God stooped low, not for applause, but out of obedience. If our ministry is not grounded in love, it will eventually show in our attitude, our words, our relationships, and our results.

Honest Questions for Every Servant of God

Self-examination is necessary if we are to avoid serving from the wrong motives. Consider these questions:

- Are we preaching to make an impact or to gain a following? If the goal is simply to draw a crowd, then the focus has shifted from Christ to self.
- Are we giving to truly bless others or to build an image? If giving is done so that others will notice, then it loses its spiritual value before God.
- Are we leading because we are called or because we crave attention? Leadership that comes from craving recognition is self-serving and will not last.

When service is pursued for selfish reasons, comparison begins to take root. Leaders start chasing titles instead of transformation. People begin to operate in the flesh rather than in the Spirit. However, when the heart is pure, God's anointing is evident, and lasting fruit begins to grow. Recognition from people may never come, but the greatest reward is hearing the Lord say, "Well done."

Ministry from a Pure Heart Produces Lasting Fruit

The difference between fruitful ministry and flashy ministry lies in the heart. A ministry that grows from purity bears fruit that endures. But the ministry done for attention fades quickly when applause fades. God is not impressed by numbers, platforms, or eloquence. He is looking for faithfulness. He seeks those who will serve when no one notices, give when no one claps, and obey when no one cheers.

When ministry flows from a surrendered heart, it becomes life-giving rather than life-draining. It heals instead of hurts, builds instead of divides, and glorifies God instead of man. Leaders who operate from this place are not driven by ego but led by the Spirit. They are not performing for people but serving from a deep love for the Father.

This requires constant heart checks. Before every sermon, every song, every meeting, and every act of service, we must ask God to purify our motives. We must allow Him to prune areas that crave affirmation and replace them with a renewed sense of purpose and peace. True joy and fulfillment in ministry are found in God's approval, not in human applause.

Final Word

There is no shame in checking the heart. In fact, it is a necessity. Ministry is too holy to be handled carelessly, too sacred to be misused for personal gain. Ministry is not about us. It is about Him. And when we shift the focus back to Him, He takes care of everything else.

If you have ever found yourself serving for the wrong reasons, you are not alone. Many of us have stumbled in this area. But God is gracious, offering us the opportunity to realign, repent, and return to Him with a pure heart. Do not let your gift outgrow your character, and do not let applause replace the anointing. Serve with clean hands and a pure heart, allowing God to shape your motives.

Make this your prayer: "Create in me a clean heart, O God, and renew a right spirit within me" (Psalm 51:10). When you pray this earnestly, God will align your heart with His, and your ministry will bear fruit that honors Him and impacts lives for eternity.

Lesson 54
Lessons from the Book of Job

Scripture: Job 1:6 thru 12

The book of Job invites us to wrestle with some of life's hardest questions about suffering, weakness, and the limitations of human existence. It challenges us to consider why we should continue to trust God even when life feels unfair or when everything seems to be falling apart. The book addresses two of the most pressing issues for all people: the problem of suffering and the sovereignty of God. It reminds us that God is still in control even when we cannot make sense of our circumstances. Job's life demonstrates that the righteous are not immune to trials, and his example continues to teach us how faith can endure through the darkest of seasons.

At the heart of Job's story lies a central question: Can a righteous person hold on to faith in God when everything goes wrong? To read Job is to discover that he was more than a wealthy man; he was a worshipper of God, a faithful husband, a devoted father, and a man of great integrity. He feared the Lord and sought to live in a way that honored Him. One of Job's most admirable qualities was his devotion as a father. He made it a regular practice to intercede for his children, lifting them in prayer and offering sacrifices on their behalf. His faith was not shallow or seasonal. It was consistent, intentional, and deeply rooted in his love for God and his family.

Lesson I: Parents Pray and Intercede on Behalf of Your Children

Job chapter 1 reveals that Job consistently interceded for his children, praying for them and offering burnt offerings to God in case they had sinned (Job 1:5). His actions remind us that parents have not only the responsibility of raising their children physically and emotionally, but also the spiritual duty of covering them in prayer. In today's world, where children are constantly exposed to temptation and pressure, the need for intercession is even greater.

It truly does take a village to raise a child, but it also takes a village of believers who are willing to stand in the gap through prayer. Parents who pray over their children establish a spiritual foundation that will remain with them even when they are older. Proverbs 22:6 assures us that when children are trained in the way they should go, they will not depart from it. Likewise, Ephesians 6:4 reminds parents to raise their children in the nurture and admonition of the Lord. Children who are surrounded by prayer are more likely to remember and return to the faith they were raised in, even when they stray.

Lesson II: All Believers in God Are Targets of Satan

Job's story also shows us that every believer is a target of Satan. Job 1:8–12 reveals how Satan sought permission to attack Job, and God allowed the trial to prove Job's faithfulness. Likewise, 1 Peter 5:8 reminds us that the devil prowls around like a roaring lion seeking whom he may devour. Believing in God, striving to live a holy life, attending church faithfully, participating in ministry, and even giving tithes and offerings do not exempt us from Satan's attacks.

In fact, the more faithful a believer is, the more determined Satan becomes to tear them down. Our faith and obedience put us on the enemy's radar, making us prime targets for discouragement and destruction. But even in this truth, we find encouragement: Satan is not more powerful than God, and his attacks are limited by God's sovereign hand.

Lesson III: None, the Unjust nor the Just, Are Exempt from Suffering

Job was known as a righteous man, yet he suffered deeply on every level: mentally, physically, and spiritually. Mentally, he suffered because he lost everything he owned, including his children and possessions, in a single day (Job 1:13–19). Physically, he endured terrible affliction when his body was covered with painful boils (Job 2:7). Spiritually, he experienced a season when he could not sense God's presence and longed to find Him (Job 23:3).

Job's story illustrates that suffering is not always the result of sin. Even the righteous will experience pain, loss, and confusion. Job 14:1 reminds us that man born of woman is of few days and full of trouble, while John 16:33 assures us that trials will come, but Christ has already overcome the world. Suffering is part of the human condition, and none of us is exempt.

Lesson IV: You Can Endure Trials and Tribulations If You Know Where Your Blessings Come From

Job was able to endure his trials because he knew the source of his blessings. When everything was taken from him, he declared, "The Lord gave, and the Lord hath taken away; blessed be the name of the Lord" (Job 1:21). His trust was not in his wealth, health, or even his family. It was in God. Even in his pain, he declared in Job 13:15, "Though he slay me, yet will I trust in him."

Trusting God allows us to endure life's trials and tribulations. When we remember that every blessing we enjoy comes from the Lord, we can hold on to our faith even when those blessings are removed. The God who gives has the authority to take away, and He also has the power to restore. It is this understanding that sustained Job and can sustain us as well.

Final Word

The book of Job teaches us that trusting God in the midst of suffering brings blessings on the other side of the trial. Job's faith was tested beyond what many of us could imagine, but his trust in God never completely wavered. In the end, God rewarded his faithfulness, blessing him with twice as much as he had before (Job 42:10–12).

When trials come, we must remind ourselves that suffering is not the end of the story. God is sovereign, and He is faithful. He sees our pain, hears our prayers, and honors our trust in Him. If we hold on, even in the darkest seasons, we too will discover that God can restore, renew, and bless us beyond measure.

Lesson 55
Restoring A Broken Nation

Scripture: II Kings 5:1 and 14

We all can acknowledge that America today is a broken nation. The signs are all around us: on the television news, over the radio, and across social media platforms. At every level, from national to state to local, we see dysfunction and division. Corrupt political parties and politicians, prejudiced leaders and citizens, ego-driven officials, hateful and mean-spirited people, and broken families have all contributed to the weakening of our nation's moral and spiritual fabric. Even within the church, scandals and unfaithful leadership have added to the sense of brokenness. The once-proud land of the free and home of the brave is in desperate need of repair and restoration.

We live in a nation that is not only economically fractured but also spiritually wounded. The economy is unstable, health care is unaffordable for many, and our communities of faith are weakened by internal strife. Consider a few examples: requirements for good jobs are higher than ever, yet wages are disproportionately low. Those who need health care most are unable to afford it because the costs are outrageous. Government decisions have threatened public education while directing funds toward private institutions. The crime rate continues to rise, and racism remains an ugly reality as people are still judged by the color of their skin rather than the content of their character.

The saddest reality is that many of those in power refuse to admit that America is broken. Leaders turn a blind eye to the moral decline and justify their actions by doing what seems right in their own eyes rather than what God requires (Judges 21:25). For this reason, the call to restoration must begin not with politics, but with repentance and obedience to God.

How Can a Broken Nation Be Restored?

Restoring a broken nation requires repairing the heart and mindset of its leadership and its people. The narrative of II Kings 5 gives us timeless principles through the story of Naaman, the commander of the Syrian army. Naaman was a man of great reputation, a mighty man of valor, highly honored, and with an impressive résumé. Yet behind his accomplishments was a deep flaw: he was afflicted with leprosy. Though he was powerful, wealthy, and respected, he lived with brokenness. His story reminds us that titles and accolades do not make a person righteous, nor do they exempt anyone from trials, suffering, or sin.

When we study Naaman's journey, we see that broken lives and even broken nations can be restored, but only when certain steps are taken.

Lesson I: Acknowledgment Is the First Step to Restoration

A nation cannot be healed if it refuses to admit that it is broken. In II Kings 5:1, Naaman is introduced with all his great qualities, yet the verse concludes with a devastating truth: "but he was a leper." His greatness was overshadowed by his brokenness. Likewise, America cannot experience restoration until leaders and citizens alike confess their flaws and acknowledge the depth of the nation's moral and spiritual sickness.

David modeled this acknowledgment in Psalm 51:1-3 when he prayed for God to have mercy on him, blot out his transgressions, wash him thoroughly, and cleanse him from his sin. In verse 3, David confessed openly that he could not escape his sin. In the same way, restoration for a nation or individual begins with humility and confession. When we acknowledge our weakness, brokenness, and sins, God promises restoration.

Lesson II: Restoration Requires Seeking Help from the Righteous

Naaman's healing came through the advice of his wife's maid, who recognized the seriousness of his condition and suggested he seek out the prophet of Israel for help (II Kings 5:2–6). She did not point him to a doctor or an earthly professional but to a man of God. This shows us that deliverance and healing often come through spiritual channels, not worldly ones.

281

In the same way, a broken nation cannot be healed by unrighteous leaders or self-serving policies. True restoration comes when the unrighteous connect with the righteous, when a nation seeks God's guidance through His people. Lawyers, doctors, and political figures have their roles, but the ultimate healing comes from the Lord. Just as Naaman needed the prophet to point him to God, our nation must seek direction from righteous voices who will connect us to the Great Physician who never loses a patient.

Lesson III: Restoration Requires Humility and Obedience to Godly Instruction

Naaman nearly missed his healing because of pride. In II Kings 5:11-12, he became angry when told to wash seven times in the Jordan River. He expected Elisha to heal him dramatically, and when his expectations were not met, he left angry and complaining. Pride blinded him to the simple obedience required for his healing.

This mirrors our nation today. Too often, leaders and citizens allow pride, arrogance, and self-interest to block the path to restoration. Solomon warned in Proverbs 16:18 that pride goes before destruction, and a haughty spirit before a fall. Pride will always hinder God's work of deliverance.

Thankfully, Naaman eventually humbled himself. In II Kings 5:13-14, he obeyed the prophet's instructions, dipped seven times in the Jordan, and his flesh was restored like that of a child. His obedience brought healing. In the same way, nations and individuals must lay aside pride, submit to God's Word, and follow His instructions if restoration is to take place.

Final Word

God is still in the business of restoring broken nations and broken lives. Just as He restored Naaman, He can restore America and every other nation that will humble itself and seek Him. Restoration will not come through pride, politics, or human strategies but through confession, repentance, humility, and obedience.

If leaders and citizens acknowledge their brokenness, seek help from the righteous, and humbly obey God's Word, restoration is possible. America may be fractured, but it is not beyond repair. The same God who healed Naaman can heal our land, if we trust Him, obey Him, and allow Him to guide us toward renewal.

About the Author

Bishop Mays is the son of the First Baptist Church (Coolwell) in Amherst, Virginia. He was licensed to preach at the age of 15 in 1968 and ordained in 1971 to Pastor the Pine Hill Baptist Church, Arrington, Virginia, under the leadership of his beloved late Pastor, the Rev. J.P. Rose.

Bishop Marshall D. Mays is the Pastor of the Otterville Baptist Church, Bedford, Virginia, the Ivy Hill and St. Paul Baptist Churches, Amherst, Virginia. He formerly served as Pastor of the Pine Hill Baptist Church, Arrington, Virginia, and the Union Hill Baptist Church, Amherst, Virginia.

He serves as Vice President of Academic Affairs at the Virginia University of Lynchburg Leonard N. Smith School of Religion.

Bishop Mays has been a lifelong learner and lover of higher academia. His early education occurred in the Amherst County Public School System. He is the recipient of the following degrees: the Associate of Arts in Liberal Arts and Sciences, the Bachelor of Arts in Theology, the Master of Divinity, and the Doctor of Ministry from Virginia University of Lynchburg. He is also a graduate of Eastern Theological Seminary with a Master of Religious Education Degree. As a result of his commitment to education and ministry, he is the recipient of two honorary degrees and numerous awards. In addition, he has had post-graduate study at Liberty University.

Dr. Mays was elevated and consecrated as Bishop of Education of the Ecumenical Global Mission Alliance Reformation, Bishop Carol Baltimore, Presiding Prelate, on Saturday, April 5, 2024, in Baltimore, Maryland.

Bishop Mays has served as the President of the Mt. Pleasant Baptist Sunday School Convention of Central Virginia and Moderator of the Peaks of Otter Baptist Association, Bedford, Virginia, and the Rockfish Baptist Association of Central Virginia, and Head of the Moderator's Council of the Virginia Baptist State Convention. He also has served as Advisor for the Deacons and Deaconess Ministry and Assistant Statistician of the Virginia Baptist State Convention.

Bishop Mays is presently serving a second tenure as Moderator of Peaks Otter Baptist Association, Bedford, Virginia. He is the author of three books: *"Decently and In Order: An Administrative Handbook and Guide for Small and Rural Churches," "Decently and In Order: A Study Guide for the Deacon and Deaconess,"* and *"Serving Together: Pastors and Deacons in Cooperation, Not Conflict."*

Bishop Mays is married to the former Florence McDaniel, and he is the father of five daughters and the grandfather of ten grandchildren and two great-grandchildren.

Made in the USA
Columbia, SC
20 January 2026

77763521R00163